Home Staging In Tough Times

By Barbara Jennings, CSS/CRS
Academy of Staging and Redesign

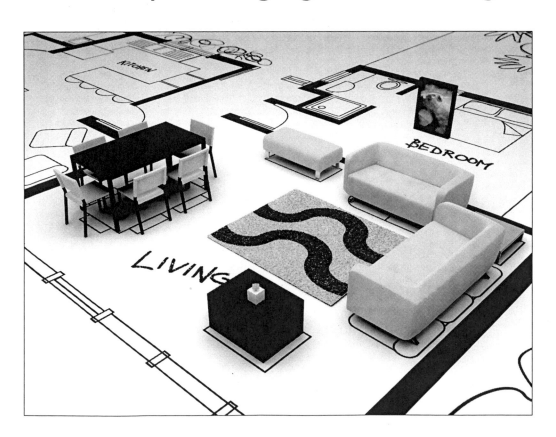

Table of Contents

Chapter One
A New Mind Set for Tough Times

Millions of people have been, or will be, thrown out of work during economic down turns – this has been true in the past and it is presently true and will also  be true in the future. For many, the prospects for new employment in economic upheaval are dismal, if not completely impossible, especially if coupled with a lack of experience or too much experience, lack of knowledge or too much knowledge, their age, their sex, their ethnicity or a multitude of other reasons. Others may also have experienced a divorce or death in the family that has caused additional financial turmoil to surface. Still others have never had a career or are changing careers and this alone has caused financial stress to creep into their lives. From this group and even the population as a whole, a Harris Poll found that 37% of those surveyed were considering or were already running a business of their own or looking to maximize their assets or learning how to monetize what they already have or could have during tough times. For many people the answer lies in starting or acquiring a business of their own.

Regarding current business owners, what isn't clear is whether the majority of these entrepreneurs consider their business as an opportunity or as a necessity. So before we get into the specifics of running a home staging or redesign business in tough times, there is one very specific ingredient you **absolutely must have** if you intend to be successful – that ingredient is **passion**. Without passion you will probably fail – even in a good economy. If you are not excited about what you offer, no one else will be excited about it either.

But let's stop a moment and define passion as it relates to what I will be discussing. I'm not just talking about being enthusiastic. When I speak about the subject of passion, I'm talking about having a passion, in everything you do, to help make someone else's life better. This will be the theme throughout this guide – helping you to become more successful is <u>my</u> passion. But you also must have a passion for helping other people get what they want or to get what they need.

Your customer (or rather your <u>client</u>) must be your first focus – your only focus. If your focus is on you and what you will get from a transaction, you may succeed in spite of yourself, but you will never achieve the true rewards and the highest and best potential you have before you. Study highly successful business people and you will find that they have one thing in common – they <u>care</u> about their clients or customers. They treat others the way they would want to be treated. So let's do one thing from the outset. When referring to the people we do business with, let's always refer to them as "clients" rather than "customers". The very essence of the word "client" carries a much more personal feeling – a feeling more akin to someone we are giving advice to for their enrichment or profit or betterment. The word "customer" is far less personal.
A retail establishment, such as a store or restaurant, caters to customers. But we are consultants and consultants serve clients.

To be truly successful as a consultant, you must adopt the mindset of treating your clients as truly valued members of your own family. You should have the desire to always do what is in their best interest over and above your own. You should seek to befriend them, listen to them, encourage them and steer them in the right directions, even if it means you take a loss or do not make a profit. This is the core mindset you need to adopt right now if you haven't done so already. You want to strive to have your clients absolutely thrilled with your services and products. If they are, they will be enthusiastic about praising you to everyone  they know. Their enthusiasm will increase your own pleasure in your business and your good feelings about yourself and the value you bring to the marketplace. In the end, when we face our Maker, it is not going to be the amount of money we earned that He will reward us for – it is going to be the relationships we built and the ways we helped other people that will prompt Him to say, "Well done good and faithful servant."

I have shopped in Home Depot for decades. But there is something going on in Home Depot and other companies like them right now that was not there in years past. Whenever I walk into my local store, I'm greeted with a friendly smile from every employee while I am there. When I ask for something, the employee not only tells me where to find it, they escort me to the aisle and the very product itself. They disguise it by saying, "I'm going your way anyway", but I'm not fooled. They have been trained to go the extra mile to help me find what I'm looking for. And when I leave the store, they thank me for coming in – and I'm not talking about the person at the check out counter either. I'm talking about all the clerks and sales staff. It has made such an impression on me that I'm writing about them in this guide.

It is very obvious that there has been a complete shift in the way Home Depot does business – and it has started at the top and filtered down to every employee. It has become their focus – to give great service with a smile. It is obvious that it is now a part of their entire training process and drilled into every employee – at least in my local store.

This is what I'm talking about. It's a shifting of focus to what is best and most helpful to the customer – their clients – and it is having a real positive effect on shoppers. The same reaction will be seen if you devote quality time and attention to making sure your clients are well served, that they feel special by the way you have treated them and that they go away from you feeling like you really cared about them as a person – as people – and not as a profit center.

Developing a Passion for What You Do

But passion just doesn't occur. And to simply start and stop with a smile (as powerful as a smile can be) is not enough. You've got to develop a plan and carry your plan through in everything you do. Here, briefly, are 5 necessary ingredients for your overall plan:

1) **Energy** - Don't dissipate your energy by dwelling on negative issues. What you focus on is what will increase in your life. So don't focus on the economy. Don't sit around worrying about how long the cycle will last. Focus instead on the opportunity before you and the fact that you have a chance to grow or start your business when costs are lower, when you're not likely to be overwhelmed at the beginning and when marketing or advertising your business will be less expensive. Use your energy in positive, constructive and hopeful ways.

2) **Vision** - Your vision is a picture of how you're going to fulfill your purpose. Give yourself permission to succeed and stop limiting what you can accomplish. If you can earn $10,000, you can earn $100,000. If you can earn $100,000 you can earn $1,000,000 and so on and so on and so on. You've got to believe in yourself first. If you don't believe in yourself and your purpose and goals, no one else will believe in you either. It all starts with you.

3) **Worthiness of Your Purpose** - Always try to see every situation from the point of view of the other person. Speak to people about how you can help them, benefit them, encourage them, and support them. Sell what you're doing to others based on the value for them (not for you). This is not only good for business, but good for your personal life as well.

4) **Commitment** - Do not take "no" for an answer. Be on a crusade to add value to the lives of as many people as you can. Know that developing a clientele is a process: it will take time, repetitive contacts and follow up. Some clients will develop quickly or instantly. Most will take time to cultivate. If you prepare yourself for this fact, you will not become discouraged when people don't seem to respond at all.

5) **Have a Code of Conduct** - In every area of life, take the high road. Be dedicated to serving others. Be committed to excellence in all you do. Then you will command respect and loyalty from everyone you encounter in life. Never compromise your integrity. Life has a way of giving back to you what you put out there. So if you are focused on doing good things for others, life will give you good results in return. It just happens.

I have spent many years writing and developing products that I believed were superior to anything on the market in the home staging and redesign industry. My focus in writing my books has always been to give great content, detailed specifics, practical advice and a sense of personal involvement. I'm committed to giving you everything I have to give within the purpose of the book – holding nothing back – at least nothing that I am consciously aware of doing. The same goes for my website and my free discussion forum.

Now, several years later, people are coming to me and wanting to partner with me in various ways. I'm not seeking them out – they are making proposals to me. Yes, it took time and a lot of hard work to develop a reputation of value and worth, but I wouldn't have it any other way. You should not settle for less than the best you have to give or offer to others. So it is imperative that you learn all about your assets, your uniqueness, your talents and your expertise so that you can powerfully convey that to other people. To do less is not in the best interests of those other people.

When I first published some of my earlier guides, I periodically mentioned other products or books that I had developed which I believed were in my reader's best interest to know about. Unfortunately I was periodically berated for doing this and accused of merely advertising my products for self-serving gain. However, that was not my intent. I felt sincerely that it was in my client's best interest to know what else was available to help them achieve their goals. Eventually I mention these types of items solely at the end of the books (which is where you'll find them in this book as well).

Not everyone appreciates the finer points of having their awareness raised and sees everything and everyone as merely a salesperson peddling their goods to them. This is unfortunate for them, really, because without knowledge of what is currently helpful, how does one properly prepare for the onslaught of competition, market apathy, lack of market share, personal fear or reluctance and a host of other factors that contribute to one's success or failure?

When you are a giving person, and you are fair, and you focus on how you can give more and more and more of yourself, your time, your expertise, your experience, people recognize that and they naturally want to be a part of that. So I challenge you to start or to continue or to move in the direction of developing your energy, your vision, a worthy purpose, your commitment to your purpose and conducting yourself with the highest code of ethics. If you do, it won't matter too much what else you do or fail to do. You are bound to be successful – even during tough times.

What Will Help You the Most

There are other authors on the subject of building and sustaining a home staging business. While I applaud them for their contributions, I have noticed that there's tends to be a lot of rhetoric and pages upon pages of theory alone. While I have written a good deal of theory myself, I've also increasingly tried to put myself in your shoes and ask over and over and over again, this question: What do I really need to launch, grow and sustain my business – particularly if the economy or my life has suffered a downturn?

I'd like to think I'm pretty normal and the things I would want would be the same as the things you would want. Yes, I find the theory valuable, but what I really, really want are the practical tools – the scripts – the forms – the ads – everything I might possibly need to manage my business, but even more importantly, to promote my business.

I can have all the theory in the world and understand the general concepts. I can know where to put the furniture and accessories. I can have a large base of contacts and people willing to help me and mentor me and so forth.

But if I come off looking or sounding like an amateur, I'm not going to get the work. I know that when I'm new at something or feeling desperate for any reason at all, I can quickly become tongue tied and start stammering or saying that dreaded "uh . . . ." and I don't want to look and sound unprofessional. I'm betting that you don't either.

So as I've evaluated all the books I've written so far, I've decided to try to be even more practical, more specific, more helpful – more of everything – in this book because I know that's what you're looking for and I know that's what's still missing out in the marketplace.

You're not going to find a huge number of pictures in this book. If you want This book is going to be packed with what I consider the core of the solutions to how you can survive – and thrive – in this market or any market – during tough economic times – during tough personal times.

Many authors and trainers will tell you that you must join their association. Or they will tell you that you must be certified by them. Or they will tell you that you must buy their career book or portfolio or their course or class or seminar.

But the simple fact of the matter is this. You can have all that and you can purchase all of that and you can attend seminars until you're broke. None of that will mean very much at all unless you know how to promote yourself and your business. I was the first person in the industry to create "a la carte" promotional aids, resources and tools for my student's. I shattered the myth that one could only learn this business and be successful if one took an expensive seminar and joined someone's organization or group.

While all that is beneficial to one degree or another, what it all really boils down to is YOU – how you come across as a person. Do you sound scared? Do you look nervous? Do you have the right vocabulary? Do your materials look professional? Do you present your case in a logical, benefit driven manner? Do you come across as needy or self-serving? Can you answer questions authoritatively? Are your design skills up to par? How focused on the needs of your prospect or client are you? Do you have multiple streams of income or just one? How many tactical procedures do you have in place? Do you have an overriding strategy that controls and focuses and governs everything you do? How client-focused are you? What is your customer service like? What kind of guarantees do you offer? Do people like you? Do people trust you? Do you have their best interests in mind? How well do you control your activities? What is the best use of your time? What is the life time value of your client?

You see there is a lot to consider. Most books talk all around these questions but never really give you the down to earth specifics – the examples – that you can tweak for your own purposes. They want you to figure that part out for yourself or pay them more money to learn it. Since most trainers and authors have never really delved specifically in their own businesses, they lack the wisdom and knowledge to pass on to you.

I might still fall short of my goals for this manual, but it is my sincere wish that you will find the pages in this guide filled with the kind of practical aid that you are looking for. Yes, there will be more theory. But along with the theory and concepts, I've tried to give you the real essence of practicality – the kind of stuff you won't get any where else – the kind of stuff that will genuinely help you in your business, no matter what type of economy you are working in.
If you go away and succeed in any aspect of your business after reading this, the book will be a success. Your success is the only success that counts. If you don't find one or more ideas, concepts, examples, forms, ads, letters and the like helpful, then I have failed you. I don't want a single reader to miss out on benefiting from their purchase and the time and effort to read this material. I owe you the most value-filled, practical, helpful resources I can muster up and conceive for you and deliver them within these pages.

The Real Secrets to Success

After training multitude thousands of people and seeing more than my share of people quit and give up, even though I had taught them (or made available to them) far more than they should ever need to be successful, I dedicated myself to seeking even more and better solutions. I realized that while theory is excellent, most people struggle with adapting theory to their own situation. Most people find it difficult to apply what they learn no matter how eloquently the theory is expressed.

In a great thriving economy, some people explode their businesses. Others succeed in spite of themselves. But during tough times, a consultant must work harder and smarter to succeed and keep growing. In tough times one cannot leave anything to chance. And one should also look to "out of the box" methods that might become even more fruitful than the traditional methods.

That's what I'm going to attempt to address in these pages. So this book isn't going to be filled with decorating theory. It's not going to contain basic business start up know how. I've already written about design and the basics in my other books anyway.

Here I'm going to concentrate on the kind of stuff mega-careers are built on. I'm going to give you simple stuff. I'm going to give you complicated stuff. You're going to find some of it (perhaps) a bit scary. But just remember, you didn't learn to walk without falling down. You watched other people walk and gradually you imitated what you saw them doing.

As you run across examples that I've sprinkled throughout this manual, I don't want you to use them verbatim. You won't learn much if you do that. I want you to take them and strip them down and learn how to rephrase them or rework them in accordance with your unique personality. In other words, "make them yours". They've got to come across with your flavor – your style – your mindset – they've got to be YOU.

If you will do that, you should reap the corresponding rewards.

When you make them yours, you will have something that no other business in the industry has – and your competition will not know how you managed to take over your territory and become the "go to" person in your community (unless, of course, they bought this manual too). But remember, knowledge without action is pretty useless. You've got to take the concepts I give you and act upon them or you will never derive any benefit in your business.

Chapter Two
Promoting a Business in Tough Times

Business is All About Promotion

Starting a business or sustaining a business is not easy. That's why most new businesses are gone within less than 5 years. Many people fail because they chose the wrong kind of business. Others fail because they spend all their time doing the business rather than promoting the business. If you think projects are just going to fall into your lap, you're in for a rude awakening. That is not how business operates.

You've got to adopt the mindset that you will constantly promote your business in a wide assortment of ways. You've got to understand that promoting your business is a task that never ends. It is constant. Yes, the methods and frequency and the thrust may change, but the promotion (no matter what form it takes) must always exist.

You've got to realize that everything you say and do should, by design, constantly advance and enhance your business in the minds of others. Remember that phrase – advance and enhance – because if you are not advancing your reputation and if you are not enhancing your service or  product or offer in the minds of your prospects and clients, then your business is moving backwards and may not survive.

You've heard the saying, "When the going gets tough, the tough get going." In tough times you've got to be especially cagey; you've got to be especially adept;

you've got to be especially wise about how you advance and enhance your business. In tough times, most businesses cut back on their promotions due to lack of revenue or fear. Lack of revenue should never be a reason for pulling back one's promotions because you don't need cash to promote your business. You do need adaptability. You do need a mind shift. You do need to refocus. But you can still advance and enhance your business no matter how tough it gets.

In Chapter Five are a number of forms that will help you dissect your personal strengths, your talents, your assets, your trade-able goods and services, identify your contacts, identify the types of businesses you could trade with, and a host of other factors you must identify if you want to truly gain the most you can gain from this guidance.

I know, I know, I know. You don't like to fill out forms. You don't want to do anything more than just read on. You don't want to have to do anything at all. You just want to fill your mind with more information and knowledge but acting on this knowledge isn't part of the plan.

If that's how you feel, then put this book down now and read no further. Because it is not in your best interest to waste any more of your time if you're not going to follow through and act upon the guidance in the most powerful ways possible. I know this is probably your first reaction because I've trained enough people through the years to understand that few people actually take action, no matter what they learn.

I also know this may be your reaction because I've been there myself. I've studied countless books and courses, listened to countless tapes, CDs and watched videos and DVDs, and even though I'm definitely an action oriented person, even I have failed to act on a wide variety of issues that I have been advised to act upon. It is human nature to put things off. It is human nature to let other lesser activities take up so much time we don't have time to do what we really ought to do.

I also know that it is easy to make excuses for why we should not do something – particularly when it comes to filling out forms. It might not be fun. It can be tedious. It makes us think – and we're already tired of thinking.

But I can assure you (from my own personal experience) that filling out the forms will open your eyes. It will open your mind. It will help you see things about yourself and your business that you presently do not see. These forms are not to be filled out completely in one sitting. They are to be started. You are to keep them handy and add to them each day for several weeks (even months).

You have my permission to make photo copies of the forms so that you keep a fresh, blank set in the book. Staple them together or put them in a binder or folder. You will not be able to think of all the information at one time, so don't feel compelled to sit for hours pondering over them. But start on them. They will ultimately reveal so much to you it will surprise you – no, it will astonish you. So briefly, let's discuss the forms I'm providing to you.

The Broadbrush Assessment of Your Business

This form will help you analyze every aspect of your business as it currently exists. Do not fill this out until the end because it is a summary of the information you will collect on the other forms.

Optimal Model Questionnaire

This form helps you analyze your goals and directions. It also helps you identify your strengths and weaknesses, determine where you focus should be and why, help you prioritize your tasks, tactics and strategies.

Six Bartering Opportunity Lists

You'll be making both personal lists and business lists. In part this is because you may need to or want to practice in the personal realm before committing your business. Or you may need to generate some quick cash and it can often be easier to do this in the personal realm. Each form asks for slightly different information, so don't think they are all the same and neglect doing any of them.

Your True Asset List

Assets can be tangible or intangible. It doesn't matter. They are all valuable and can be traded for what you need or want, both personally and in business.

Your Skill List

Throughout your life you have developed a set of skills which you may or may not be using in your business, only because you never thought about their worth and how you could use them. These skills will be part of you to different degrees. Some skills will be polished and perfected skills. Others will be moderately perfected. They will have less value probably, but they are none the less valuable in some form or to someone.

Your Knowledge List

Your knowledge has probably evolved into some kind of expertise in some areas. In other areas you have familiarity with topics. To lesser or greater degrees, your knowledge can be a valuable asset that you could use to your advantage to benefit someone else.

Twelve Relationship Lists

You'll notice there are 12 forms in this category. Each one is a little different and will help you pull out all of the obvious and not so obvious relationships you have developed through the years that you are or are not aware of right now. Spend a lot of time on these lists. Keep adding to them. These lists will be a gold mine for you once you have fully developed them. They include both your personal relationships as well as business relationships.

Three Yellow Page Research Lists

You will want to develop these lists a little later on. These lists will help you target businesses in your local area that could be prime candidates for you to trade with using the bulk of your assets, skills and knowledge. Any product or service that you normally have to pay cash for currently can be revised into a barter or trade, releasing you from spending your cash and developing business for you that could eventually turn into cash transactions down the road when better times return.

Actual Barter Scrip for Staging and Redesign

I've created three forms for you to use in place of "money". They are each one page long – simple agreements – not scary, lengthy documents full of legalese that scare people off. Don't think they are not binding in court – they are – but they are simple to execute and simple to understand. If you prefer to create your own, be my guest. These should help you develop Scrip more to your liking or to customize for your own purposes.

Due Bill

This agreement covers transactions you wish to make that will be fulfilled in the future as opposed to those to be transacted (at least on one side) in the here and now. Feel free to adapt it to your own purposes.

Disclaimer

I am not an attorney. These Scrips and other forms are presented as samples and I in no way guarantee them as being complete, nor do I guarantee they will protect your rights in actuality or in a court of law. You use them at your own risk. To make sure your agreements adhere to the laws where you live, please get advice from a qualified attorney you trust.

Once You Complete Your Lists and Forms

If you have taken the time to fill out the valuable forms in this manual, you are to be congratulated. I am confident that you have identified a ton of information about yourself, your business, your community, your assets (both tangible and intangible), your intrinsic value, your direction, your goals and where you feel you can best improve your tactics and strategies for the greatest benefit of your clients and your bank account.

So at this point I'm going to assume you have identified some people or business contacts that you wish to introduce your offers to. You may also be feeling apprehension about that. I know for myself I have always had to battle the reluctance of picking up the phone and talking with strangers. I'm very shy, you see, and often concerned about how I come across, especially if I have to "wing" it on the phone or in person when I am not as prepared as I would like to be.

Happily you do not need to introduce yourself to people initially in ways that scare you or make you feel intimidated. I have always found it helpful to send a letter of introduction first, and then follow up with a phone call or other means of communication. If you are really apprehensive, you can find someone who is good at this and hire them to do it for you, but I recommend you challenge yourself to meet your fears and conquer them.

When I first started out in business I was completely frozen in my tracks and couldn't even walk into a business and ask for a business card. I'm betting you're not that weak. As a young adult, I had to have my father go with me just to find out if a company was hiring or not. That's pretty serious fear. But over the years I've forced myself to confront my fears, and while I will admit I have not vanquished them, I certainly have learned to do many things I never thought I would be able to do. You can too. Give yourself time. Take each step. To help you ease into it, I've prepared a sample letter of introduction you can use as a pattern or to help give you ideas of what you can write in your own letter.

Sample Letter of Introduction

For those of you who are more comfortable making your opening introduction by letter rather than by phone or in person, here is a sample letter that you could send out first. Choose the owner or leading real estate agent (or broker) when writing to a real estate office. You always want to start at the top if you can, because the person at the top has the power to hire you and pass you on to anyone in the organization. The person at the top makes things happen.

You'll need to alter the letter to fit your personality, your background and experience level. But this is an excellent way to make the first impact. But please note, that no matter how good your letter is, or how powerfully you impress the recipient, you've got to follow up.

It used to be that one could write a good letter and get a good percentage of recipients picking up the phone to call back. But that isn't true anymore. Now people are busier than ever. They are overwhelmed with email. They get tons of junk mail. They mean to get back to you, but they just don't get around to it.

So while you give them a chance to contact you, you've got to keep the initiative and know that you've got to contact them again – and again – and again – and again. Studies have shown that most people need to be contacted 9-11 times before they finally do business with a company. Yet most consultants give up after only 2 tries.

So do not rely on a single letter to do the trick for you. Marketing is a sequence of steps – and if you're not prepared to follow a sequence, it's probably better not to start at all. I recently sent out 11 letters to companies, and received back only one response. Even that, quite frankly, is almost more than I expected. So now I am following up by both email and by phone as the next step. And depending on the responses at that time, more steps will be added and needed before any deals will develop.

Following, then, is a sample letter of introduction:

> "Dear _____,
>
> You may not know of me, but my name is well known to people locally in the home staging or real estate staging business arena.
>
> I'm particularly adept at explaining, demonstrating, elaborating and defining how to prepare a home to appeal to the greatest number of potential buyers – and how to gain a buyer's instant interest in the property, regardless of its value.
>
> I've looked at your business from afar and have seen something very, very potentially lucrative that you might not have seen yet. If I'm at all correct, very conservatively speaking, it could be worth an extra $100,000 + a year in newfound income. Again, if my premise is correct, it should be sustainable for years to come.
>
> In a depressed economy, it becomes essential to look for additional ways to improve on the tactics and strategies that have worked in the past. I'm sure you would agree that procedures can always be improved.
>
> I would like to more fully discuss and explain my services to you, and I'm willing to do it without even binding you to any agreement. I am probably the one best suited to make this happen, both because I understand the dynamics, and I have the skill set and the experience to back me up.
>
> It requires virtually no effort and no risk on your part. I would be doing 99% of the work. You would have total control of starting or stopping whenever you like. You and I would share in the profits, with you getting an attractive share of the revenue generated for doing practically nothing. It's the perfect passive income for you.
>
> Again, it could be very lucrative – even in this market. If what I have written intrigues you and you would like to talk further in detail, call me at (____) _____. I look forward to hearing from you soon. If I do not hear from you, I will contact you in a few days to follow up.
>
> Regards,

On the following pages I'm providing you with some more sample letters. Please note at the top of each letter who the intended recipient is and who the sender is. They are not all alike and are not to be used unless appropriate.

These are only samples and not meant to be used verbatim. As always, you need to adapt them to your personal style and manner of speaking and writing – otherwise they will be out of balance with the real you and that could be obvious once you get a chance to talk to the recipient.

In addition, you want your letters to be personalized – not canned. It would not do at all for you to send out a letter that some other reader of this manual has already sent to your list. So be sure to rewrite all of these letters in your own words – or just use them as an idea builder to creating your own unique letters.

Again, let me emphasize that as good as a letter might be, you must know that most people will not respond and it is up to you to follow up with them. It's not necessarily that they are not interested. Some won't be interested at all. Some won't be interested right now. And some may be interested, but just can't or don't wish to take the time to act now for any number of reasons. But if you never contact them again, by whatever means you choose to, then you will lose out for sure.

Within the process, each time you make contact you want to "advance and enhance" your offer or your reputation. You want to "advance and enhance" the benefits they will get from doing business with you. You want to enhance and advance their business in some way or their ability to understand yours.

Sample Introductory Letter to Agent From Stager

(NOTE: Only for use by bona fide Certified Staging Specialists who have earned my designation)

Dear _____,

Ever wonder why some homes "implode" on the market?

The reason I am writing you this letter is to inform you of the effort, expertise, knowledge and commitment to home staging services I offer that can keep many a home from suffering a languishing stay on the market forcing the owners to sell short of their goals.

Statistics over many years have proven that home staging is a key component to getting multiple offers on a home and selling a home quickly, especially in this difficult market. Home staging is the art of preparing a home visually to appeal to the broadest number of prospective buyers. Done correctly, it has often been the key ingredient in a successful, profitable, quick sale.

While other stagers probably claim great pricing, service and quality, I want to point out that I am <u>uniquely prepared to go the extra mile over and above the norm</u> and that my commitment cannot be overstated.

I went the extra mile when I got certified. While most home stagers purchased their "credentials" by attending a seminar or class, I spent untold hours studying for a rigid exam, which I passed. Then I submitted a portfolio of my work for review by a national expert in the field. I'm proud to be a Certified Home Staging Specialist through the Academy of Staging and Redesign, directed by national best selling author and expert, Barbara Jennings. Only the very top people in the industry meet her demanding standards.

For this reason, you can be confident I will bring a higher level of dedication to my work on behalf of you and your clients. <u>My goal is to make you look good – and I will work extremely hard to help your clients maximize the profits that lie hidden in their home.</u>

Because of this, I feel you have three choices when it comes to the stager you select to manage your future listings.

1) You can hire a different stager (or none at all), and they may let you down because of lack of knowledge, training and experience, forcing your clients to sell for $_____ under market and "implode" their only chance of success.

2) Or you can trust somebody else, who is in such a hurry to do the deal that they take short cuts, make ill-advised suggestions or waste your client's resources.

3) Or you can take it upon yourself and put me in touch with them - because your clients are important to you, and you trust and revere the relationship you have established with them and you want their lives to be enriched.

I just want to remind you that I will take care of your clients in the same professional manner I would do if they were my parents, best friends or neighbors.

I'm enclosing a few business cards for you to pass on to them and I would be more than happy to meet with you at any time to see how I might benefit you.

But more than that, I believe your current clients would sincerely appreciate it if you would take a small amount of time and contact them <u>for their sake</u>, so that we can all work together to bring about a successful sale. Our mutual goal would be to "explode" their profits and maximize the window of opportunity they currently have.

I will contact you in a few days to arrange a brief meeting so we can discuss the ways I can be of service to you and your clients.

Warm regards,

Sample Letter to Real Estate Agents from Stager

Dear _____,

I want to create for you a whole new under-utilized or never-utilized part of your business.

I want to do all the work, and I want you to get maximum profits and maximum credit because of it.

I have a really cool model that few people know about which I believe can be very meaningful to you. I have received extensive training in staging techniques and am confident it will help you immediately and be repeatable and profitable for as long as you wish to continue.

It can only add, not take away, from the revenue that you are currently generating and put a lot more profit in your pocket as well as your client's pockets.

I will call you in a few days to set up a brief appointment to give you all the details and allow you the opportunity to evaluate me face to face.

Warm regards,

Sample Letter to Real Estate Agents from Stager

Dear _____,

Does your client's home embarrass you?

Wouldn't you agree that if your client's home is embarrassing to you that it will inhibit you from being enthusiastic about showing it to potential buyers and their agents?

And do you find it difficult to express your concerns to your clients for fear of alienating them and ruining the good relationship you have built with them to date?

Let me be the bearer of bad news in your place.

I know how to gently persuade them to get help. I know how to masterfully point out the benefits they will get by eliminating or de-emphasizing the home's flaws and accentuating its assets.

They will see me as an expert in this all important part of the process and often take suggestions readily from me that they would find hard to accept from other people.

Since you and your clients only have a short window of opportunity to make a strong impression on buyers and their agents, let me coordinate with you to garner all the profit that lies hidden in your client's house.

Preparing a house for sale is too important to trust to just anyone.

And this is my specialty.

I will call you in a few days to set up a brief appointment to give you all the details and allow you the opportunity to evaluate me face to face.

Warm regards,

Sample Letter to Real Estate Agents from Stager

Dear _____,

Do the homes you list ever embarrass you?

Wouldn't you agree that if you're embarrassed by a property your enthusiasm to represent the home diminishes greatly? Do you find it difficult to communicate sensitive critiques about your client's property?

You don't have to be the bearer of "bad news". Allow me to bear that for you.

I've been professionally trained to analyze a home inside and out and know what needs to be done to eliminate embarrassment from the property. I'm gentle in how I point out the problems and even better, I've got great ideas for how to solve them.

I know without a doubt that I can turn minimize the negative and maximize the positive on your properties.

This is great for your client. This is great for you.

My services are very affordable, very professional and very do-able.

I will call you in a few days to set up a brief appointment to give you all the details and allow you the opportunity to evaluate me face to face.

Warm regards,

Sample Letter to Real Estate Agents from Stager

Dear _____,

There's another buyer waiting for every house – and they're too smart to buy your mistakes.

The biggest mistake your fellow agents are making is allowing their clients to put a house up for sale that isn't ready to be shown.

Less than 6% of homes on the market are actually presentable and ready to be shown to the buying public. This is great news for smart agents who have an edge over the rest of the crowd. But with foreclosures mounting, the matter of getting a house to stand out in the crowd becomes doubly hard, even when good tactics are utilized.

That's why you can't afford to trust untrained, ill-equipped, so-called professionals who do not have your client's best interests in mind, who take short cuts, and who don't understand what you're up against.

My certification process demanded I prove my knowledge and talents first to a prominent organization. Therefore my designation is one of the most respected credentials in the industry.

<u>So you can be assured any task you give to me will be professionally managed.</u> I pride myself in giving **more** than I promise, standing **behind** what I do, delivering **everything** I said I would deliver and **meeting** all deadlines I agreed to meet.

You only have a short window of opportunity to make a strong impression on buyers and their agents. **Preparing the house for sale is too important to trust to just anyone.**

I will call you in a few days to set up a brief appointment to give you all the details and allow you the opportunity to evaluate me face to face.

Warm regards,

Sample Referral Letter to Agent From Stager

Dear _____,

It's been a while since I assisted you in selling the home of your client at

_____.

The reason I am writing you this letter is to reaffirm with you the effort, expertise, knowledge and staging services I gave you that no one else could or would.

Isn't it true that because of the staging I did and the strategies I advised, that even though you originally thought your clients would have to settle for $_____, we assisted the home to generate $_____?

Isn't it true that we presented their home in such a way as to ensure that it appealed to the most prospective buyers, that buyers made higher offers than expected, and that we helped create a buying frenzy?

Because of this, I feel you have three choices <u>when it comes to your friends and your new and past clients</u> who may be wishing to sell their homes in the near future.

1) You can allow them to hire a different stager (or none at all), and they may let your friend down because of lack of knowledge, training and experience, forcing your friend to sell for $_____ under market.

2) Or you can allow that friend to trust somebody else, who is in such a hurry to do the deal that they take short cuts, make ill-advised suggestions or waste your friend's resources.

3) Or you can take it upon yourself to put them in touch with me, because that friend is important to you, and you trust and revere the friendship and you want their life to be enriched.

I just want to remind you that I will take care of your friends in the same professional manner I dealt with you and past clients, with great attention to detail, and with total commitment to what is best for them and you. I'm enclosing a few business cards for you to pass on. But more than that, I believe your friends and clients would sincerely appreciate it if you would take a small amount of time and contact them for their sake, so that they have opportunity to maximize the sale of their home too.

Warm regards,

Sample Referral Letter to Buyer From Agent

Dear _____,

It's been a while since I assisted you in purchasing your home.

The reason I am writing you this letter is to reaffirm with you the effort, expertise, knowledge and representation I gave you that no one else could or would.

Isn't it true that because of the work I did and the strategies I advised, that even though you thought you'd have to pay out $_____, instead by using the strategies we worked out together, and me holding true and you respecting me for it, we saved you an extra $_____?

Isn't it true that we purchased your home in such a way as to ensure that it did not fall out of escrow, that I preserved your intangible pleasure of a quick process and that I facilitated your ability to coordinate everything with the sale of your prior property?

Because of this, I feel you have three choices when it comes to your friends who may be wishing to sell or purchase a home.

1) You can allow your friend to list his or her home with somebody else, and they may let your friend buy for $_____ over market or sell out for $_____ under market.

2) Or you can allow that friend to trust somebody else, who is in such a hurry to do the deal that it gets all tangled up in escrow and falls out.

3) Or you can take it upon yourself to put them in touch with me, because that friend is important to you, and you trust and revere the friendship and you want their life to be enriched.

I just want to remind you that I will take care of your friends in the same professional manner I dealt with you, with great attention to detail, and with total commitment to what is best for them.

I'm enclosing a few business cards for you to pass on. But more than that, I would sincerely appreciate it if you would take a small amount of time and contact your friends for their sake, so that they have opportunity to maximize the sale or purchase of a home.

Warm regards,

Sample Referral Letter to Seller From Agent

Dear _____,

It's been a while since I assisted you in selling your home.

The reason I am writing you this letter is to reaffirm with you the effort, expertise, knowledge and representation I gave you that no one else could or would.

Isn't it true that because of the work I did and the strategies I advised, that even though you thought you'd have to settle for $_____, instead by using the strategies we worked out together, and me holding true and you respecting me for it, we got you an extra $_____?

Isn't it true that we sold your home in such a way as to ensure that it did not fall out of escrow, that I preserved your intangible pleasure of a quick process and that I facilitated your ability to purchase another residence that meets your current needs more exactly?

Because of this, I feel you have three choices <u>when it comes to your friends</u> who may be wishing to sell their homes or purchase another home.

1) You can allow your friend to list his or her home with somebody else, and they may let your friend sell out for $_____ (enter $ range) under market.

2) Or you can allow that friend to trust somebody else, who is in such a hurry to do the deal that it gets all tangled up in escrow and falls out.

3) Or you can take it upon yourself to put them in touch with me, because that friend is important to you, and you trust and revere the friendship and you want their life to be enriched.

I just want to remind you that I will take care of your friends in the same professional manner I dealt with you, with great attention to detail, and with total commitment to what is best for them.

I'm enclosing a few business cards for you to pass on. But more than that, I would sincerely appreciate it if you would take a small amount of time and contact your friends for their sake, so that they have opportunity to maximize the sale of their home (or the purchase of a different home).

Warm regards,

Sample Referral Letter to Seller From Stager

Dear _____,

It's been a while since I assisted you in selling your home. The reason I am writing you this letter is to reaffirm with you the effort, expertise, knowledge and staging services I gave you that no one else could or would.

Isn't it true that because of the staging I did and the strategies I advised, that even though you originally thought you would have to settle for $_____, I assisted the home in generating $_____?

Isn't it true that I presented your home in such a way as to ensure that it appealed to the most prospective buyers, that buyers made higher offers than expected, and that you received multiple offers for a profit of $_____?

Because of this, I feel you have three choices when it comes to your friends who may be wishing to sell their homes in the near future.

1) You can allow them to hire a different stager (or none at all), and they may let your friend down because of lack of knowledge, training and experience, forcing your friend to sell for $_____ under market.

2) Or you can allow that friend to trust somebody else, who is in such a hurry to do the deal that they take short cuts, make ill-advised suggestions or waste your friend's resources.

3) Or you can take it upon yourself to put them in touch with me, because that friend is important to you, and you trust and revere the friendship and you want their life to be enriched.

I just want to remind you that I will take care of your friends in the same professional manner I dealt with you, with great attention to detail, and with total commitment to what is best for them. I will not let you down nor embarrass you in any way.

I'm enclosing a few business cards for you to pass on. But more than that, I believe your friends would sincerely appreciate it if you would take a small amount of time and contact them for their sake, so that they have opportunity to maximize the sale of their home too.

Warm regards,

What to Do Next

What you do next will really depend on the person or business you have contacted and their reaction to your proposal. Since no two situations are the same, there is no specific "one-size fits" all response I can give you – or that anyone could give you.

What I can tell you is that if you have filled out all the forms and brought together a detailed summary of your business and your individual proposals, and you've prepared scripts for yourself for when you actually talk to your prospects, and you've made sure your prospects know that you have their best interests at heart, and you are well prepared in how you articulate what you will do for them, and you have assured them that you will do the lion's share of the work and make the whole process as easy and streamlined, as fool proof and profitable as you can make it, you should do just fine.

You won't get every deal you go after. No one does. But you'll get your fair share. And you're bound to do much better now that you've prepared more fully, that you've started thinking "outside the box", that you're finding ways to do business that are especially good during tough times, that you've opened yourself up to a new mindset, a new world view, that you're open to doing more and accepting more in your transactions.

In the forms section you'll find actual Barter Scrip you can use to transact business. You may choose to use more complicated, detailed agreements or contracts if you wish. Or you can keep things simple, straightforward and more of a "gentleman's agreement" approach.

If you're concerned about protecting your profits, whether by cash or by trade, I've written another book that covers this topic in detail and you'll find it listed at the end of this book among the other resources I also have for you.

You Must Have an Attitude of Certainty

Your attitude is very, very important. You must adopt an **attitude of certainty**.

In other words, you must believe that if you pursue an activity, a partnership, a joint venture, a business relationship – that it's just a matter of time before it will come about. It's only a matter of time before your vision becomes a tangible

31

reality. It is up to you to make it happen. It is up to you to visualize it happening. It is **not** up to the other person. It is up to you.

If you don't believe in the value of what you're doing, how can you expect anyone else to believe in it? If you don't understand all the ins and outs of what you're proposing, how can you expect anyone else to understand them?

That's not their job. They have their job already. They have achieved a small, medium or large amount of success without you. They have enough on their plate already to manage. So you come along, with your pitch, your idea, your wishes – and it means nothing to them. They've got to see how and when you will improve on what they have already established.

If you don't do a good job of showing them true value, true benefit, new income opportunities, a way to save money, a way to make even more money or save time or improve on what they're already doing, you're wasting their time and you're wasting your time.

Now before you pick up the phone to call any of the people you have written, be sure to read the next section which discusses how to get past the person who answers the phone and whose job may be to keep you from getting through to the person you want to speak with.

Sample Introduction Script to Bypass the Gatekeeper

Don't let her friendly look fool you. There are certain people in a medium or large sized entity whose sole purpose is to protect the valuable time of the person in charge. I know – I used to be one of them. I mastered the technique of screening callers and only the very best of the best got by me.

So what are you to do if you're trying to reach a top real estate agent or a broker or another highly positioned officer in a company or even trying to get past the teenager who answers the home phone? I think you'll find it effective to try to turn that person into your friend or ally first. While you'll have to reword it, here is a sample script you might use to pattern what you'd say.

> "Hello, I'm _____ with _____. I have a proposal which I think could perhaps be worth $_____, maybe $_____ a year or more to your company. I am the only person representing my company and have complete control over it.
>
> It might not be right. I'm not even certain yet if it's something I really want to do. So I especially don't want to harass you and I don't want to try to navigate around you. I realize you have a tough job to manage. I would simply like a chance to present the idea and not short circuit the important details.
>
> If necessary, I can present it to you and let you present it to your superiors, but there are complexities that make that difficult. I can work on it some more and get it down to about five minutes. If needed, I can even do it on the phone.
>
> If you'd be willing to get me just five minutes, you can come in and yank me out if I go over. And because it's such a good idea, I would personally feel bad if I ended up presenting it to somebody else just because they give me the time, when you really are my first choice."

The person might respond with, "Ok but you really need to be done in five minutes. I'm squeezing you in between meetings."

So a statement of reassurance would also be helpful:

> "I totally understand. You have my permission to pull me out. You can even shout at me, chastise me and usher me out by my ears. I just want you to know I really believe your boss will appreciate this and its value. If it doesn't have value to him, I will be out in a flash. I don't want to be anything but an asset, a benefit and a profitable resource to anyone I meet."

I have always found it beneficial to be straight with people. I respect my time and I respect their time even more. So should you.

When You Get Stuck in Voice Mail Jail

Are you one of those people who prays to get the other person's voice mail instead of having to talk to them directly? Well, get over it. You're not going to land business getting stuck forever in the voice mail jail.

Fortunately for you, there are solutions. First, you've got to make sure, on the front end, that you're totally immersed in your idea and that you can explain it inside and outside at the drop of a hat. What will you do if you get an unexpected phone call in response to one of your letters? You've got to be able to discuss your idea instantly, even when caught off guard. Until you can manage that, you shouldn't be sending out any mail. That's a given.

Secondly, you should know that leaving a voice mail can work for you if you manage it correctly. You see, most people who leave voice mail don't do it correctly. They tend to leave one of 3 different kinds of messages:

1) **They leave a foolish message**: "Hello, this is Barbara Jennings."
2) **They leave a self serving message:** "I've contacted you previously and would appreciate a response back. Please call me at _____."
3) **They leave no message at all:** Click.

Voice mail messages are always listened to by someone, so isn't it foolish to throw away the opportunity to leave a dynamic message? The problem is most people aren't truly prepared to leave a message of value. That because they think that the most valuable thing they can leave is their name and phone number. Wrong. Don't waste the opportunity for yourself.

Instead your **Attitude of Certainty** should be telling you that the person who listens to the voice mail message is most likely the very person you're trying so hard to reach. So it would behoove you to leave a fascinating message, wouldn't it? You are in a process of introducing you and your product or service of value to this person – and you have not forgotten that it is a <u>process</u> – not a one time shot.

So recognize that you are already having a progressive, intimate discussion. Yes, the give and take is delayed, but it's still a means of communication and should not be wasted or spoiled by lack of careful thought and delivery.

Make Your Message Self-Serving <u>to the Listener</u>

When the message you leave is focused on what benefits the listener, you will find your overall message is being enhanced. When you pick up the phone to call someone, you'd better be prepared to get voice mail some 70-80% of the time. If you're not expecting that, then you need a reality check. You should actually be shocked if you get a real person – that's how unlikely it has become.

You have three goals for your message.

1) You want them to call you.
2) You want to intrigue them.
3) You want them to want to listen to your next message too when you still can't get through to them.

So in that event, here is an idea of the type of message you should consider leaving when stuck in voice mail jail.

> "_____, I don't know you, but I'm acquainted with your company and it has been suggested to me that what I am doing probably is not being done by your company. The consensus of opinion is that the two or three minutes it would take for me to share it with you would probably make a bigger difference to you than me. It may or may not be something we'll ultimately do, but it's probably something you should know about. My name is _____ and my number is _____ if you'd like to contact me."

Notice that by leaving your name and number at the end of the message allows someone a chance to grab a pen and paper while you're talking so they don't have to play the message back again because they missed the contact information. You might even repeat your name and phone number at the end, just in case you spoke too quickly or some part of the message got garbled.

You probably will still not get a return call, but you've begun the process of making an interesting, intriguing phone exchange. This will help you on your next call when you still don't hear back from the recipient.

Remember, in every message you leave, you must convey your <u>attitude of certainty</u>. This is very important.

So let's take a quick peek at a possible second message:

> "_____, I was just talking with a colleague and we were discussing the application of services to another situation similar to yours, and it was about $_____. I don't think yours will be large, although I could be wrong. My colleague made me promise I would absolutely continue to pursue talking this through with you. If you're now ready to contact me, I can be reached at _____. My name is _____."

Do you see how you are continuing to advance your position? Do you see how you have enhanced it too? Each time you make a contact, by phone, by email, by letter, you continue to enhance and advance – advance and enhance.

The Force Multiplier Effect

My brother-in-law was a career officer in the US Army. In the military there is a concept called the <u>force multiplier effect</u>. What this means is that the military is divided into several entities: the army, the air force, the navy and the marines. Broken down to three basic strategies, you've got two entities that can attack by land, one entity that attacks by air and a third entity that attacks by sea. These represent the overriding **strategies** of your business.

Now within each of these military entities, you have many different **tactics** that each one will use. For instance, any single entity may use a variety of methods to attack the enemy, such as hand to hand combat, surface to air missiles, reconnaissance, covert operations, hiring guerillas to attack on their behalf, intelligence, capture and interrogation, sending out false or disinformation, infiltration and so forth.

For our purposes then, in business you also have a force multiplier effect. You've got the following methods

- Attack by land (US Mail)
- Attack by air (telephone, fax, email, text messages and online sites)
- Attack by hand to hand combat (personal face to face visits)

The latter method is the most powerful usually.

In the military, one doesn't care which strategy or tactic wins the war. They all work together and no one really cares which event was the "strike out blow". In the same manner, one really doesn't care which strategy or tactic is successful in landing the business. They all work together for a common goal.

The important thing to remember is that it is vital for success to employ more than one method of getting the business – more than one method of making contact with your prospect and more than one method of communication. Put all together, they add up to a powerful force. Given time, they will work together to bring about success, not just for you and your business, but for the other businesses you deal with too.

When your goal is to benefit the companies and home owners you deal with, and make them more successful in the process, you will come out more successful yourself. But it usually takes a process of multiple contacts in a multitude of methods to get the job done.

The longer you are in business the more you will come to see that business is war. Just when you think you have "won the battle" and your business is a huge success, that's when something unexpected comes along and challenges your success. The business climate is constantly changing, constantly evolving, constantly being affected by outside forces which cannot be predicted nor controlled.

So just as a soldier or commander has to be ever ready for the unexpected, so too does a business owner. One can never rest on the successes of the past. One can never rest on the profits of the past. And one can never rely solely on the tactics and strategies of the past.

This is another reason why it is so important to test what you are doing and be open to changing what was working with what is working, because what was working before may not ever work again – at least not as effectively.

When I began my online training company, there were a multitude of tactics that I used very effectively back then that barely work today. Likewise, the strategies I used offline decades ago don't necessarily work today. On the other hand, many strategies and tactics appearing to work well in today's market might be improved upon if one went back to strategies of the past instead. It all depends.

Let me give you an example.

It used to be that when one sent out a press release, they sent it by US mail. Everyone did it that way, so the challenge was to make your mailing piece stand out from the rest. Then it became more fashionable and effective to send out your press release by fax. So you had to have a great headline to attract attention and make your fax stand out from the rest and you needed a current list of fax numbers to send your message to. Now press releases are often sent out by email or by filling out an online form or doing an upload to someone's website or blog or twitter.

One thing is clear. Do what the majority of people are **not** doing. No one is hand delivering anything any more. So that's why you should do that very thing. Hand delivery is the oldest form of delivery going back to pioneer days (or so I've been told). By choosing routes that are no longer popular, you don't have any competition and you stand a better chance of your message getting through and being noticed.

And you also get seen.

Never discount the power of being seen in person. Your professional appearance, your countenance, your communication skills, your confidence – the whole package – you – gets seen and responded to, which is substantially more powerful than any letter, brochure, email, phone message or fax.

Use the force multiplier effect to your best advantage. Never rely on just one means of communication. Recognize that it is a process. Be willing to keep the initiative and follow the process to ultimate success.

For now, let's move on into an area of building clientele that you're probably not doing enough to take advantage. Most business owners don't think in terms of getting referrals. At best, they may only have one referral generating system in place. This is unfortunate for them. They are losing a lot of business they could have if only they took a pro-active approach to getting referrals. Don't make that mistake.

I've been discussing how to introduce yourself to "cold prospects", but it's far better if you can approach someone who is considered a "warm prospect". A warm prospect is someone who has already heard about you or has expressed an interest in hearing from you. You can send them an introductory letter too, but you can easily bypass that step if you like and make direct contact by phone to ask for an appointment. At any rate, here are some ideas to help you develop actual recurring tactics and strategies so that you always have a flow of "warm" prospects coming to you.

Using the force multiplier effect, how fast do you think your business would grow if you had a constant stream of sharp, interesting prospects handed to you on a silver platter? Well, maybe I can't quite deliver that to you myself, but you can go a long way to making that happen by concentrating quality effort into creating multiple ways of generating referrals for your business.

37 Referral Generating Ideas

In this section I'm going to give you a whole lot of ideas of how you can generate referrals for your business. These are ideas that came out of other industries, but by adapting them to our industry, you can use them effectively. A business needs to have a minimum of 5 referral generating systems. So if you're not generating referrals for yourself, you are missing out on great opportunities to build and grow your business.

1) For every nine people you send me, I'll give you
   _____ (a $200 value) plus dinner.
2) Refuse to accept their check unless they give you 5 referrals and a signed release allowing you to call the people to inquire about them hiring you for staging or redesign.
3) Give a covenant letter to non-competing companies who service homeowners and have a database. Ask the companies to endorse you to their customer list in exchange for a referral fee.

4) Join a national speakers association and become active. Members will want to do business with you and are usually good for referrals too.
5) Get a few journalists to interview your best clients. Write it up or tape the conversation with your client. Insist that you approve the name of the client and get two-way approval.
6) Get a list of all people in your county who own large property. Show the list to other rich people. If they know any of them, ask to use their name as a referral source. Or talk to your CPA or attorney. Say, "I'm not asking for a lead. I just want to know who the key wealthy people in the community are."
7) Give away a copy of your favorite book to your clients and best prospects. Contact them later to see how they liked it.
8) Get your vendors to refer you because it automatically means more business for them.
9) Conduct a small seminar about staging or redesign. Give your contacts a special discount for bringing a small number of people (3-4 guests = $_____; 5+ guests = $_____).
10) After you stage or redesign a home, use a crisscross directory and send a letter to everyone in the neighborhood saying you just "beautified their neighborhood."
11) Create a "bank of letters" and send out ten a day. Ask them to call you but also tell them that if they don't call you by a certain date that you will call them.
12) After you serve a client, send a big white cup with the words, "Thank you" imprinted on the front. Put your name on the back.
13) Remember that many people who refer you will "just want their people to be taken care of" – more than a referral fee. So make sure you really do take care of the people referred to you.
14) On the back of your envelopes print, "If there is anyone you think would benefit from the types of services I render, give us their name and address and we'll send them a free brochure."
15) Join several associations and be regular in attendance and actively participating.
16) Ask for referrals all through your process because almost everyone knows someone wanting to sell their home. Let them know a gift will come but don't tell them what it is. It could be a plant – always a nice gift.
17) Earn "thank you bucks". Get people to distribute your flyer or brochure with their "member number". When someone hires you, you send the member some "thank you bucks".
18) Look for human interest stories in the newspaper. Retell the story with your comments. Ask people to forward the story to their friends. Ask people to sign up to receive more stories. List your website at the end of the story.

19) When you call a referral say, "So and so asked me to give you a call. And I hear you're very talented at _____." Then say, "Is that true or is that just a rumor?" They should laugh. Introduce yourself last. Information to find out from the prospect: a) What they like about the person who referred you; b) What talent they do have; c) How long. Always give more than you promise.

20) At the end of a project, wait for the compliment to come and then ask for referrals. Say "Thank you so much. It has been my pleasure to serve you. You know, I don't advertise. So it's through word of mouth that I get real nice clients like you. If you have a relative, friend or co-worker that you'd like to refer to me, I'd really appreciate it and will take real good care of them."

21) Whether you are losing money on a project or not, never quit until the job is done right – and done to the client's satisfaction.

22) Send business cards to every client with their name on the back. Give a discount to any person they give the card to and give credit discount to the giver of the card.

23) Quote your price and if they buy, then you say, "I have a surprise for you. Your business has been referred to us by _____ and you get $_____ off of the price you've already negotiated and that you thought was a good price. And further, if you get to do this with one of your friends, we'll be paying you $_____ for the referral and also giving the same $_____ to your friend.

24) At the end of a project say, "Part of our fee is that I need to get five introductions from you. I need five because two will probably say "no thank you". One will be working with someone else and I'll meet with the other two. Out of the two, I'll get one or both to do business."

25) Give a strip of three postcards to your client to address and fill in and send off. Tell the client in advance that you will ask them to do this.

26) Create a valuable newsletter to send out regularly. Offer a free one year subscription to any referral.

27) Find out where your client works. Send a helium balloon to them with no advertising on it with a thank you card and referral cards or your business cards. Everyone at work will ask them if it is their birthday. They will talk about you and your service to others all day. Online companies will deliver the balloons for you.

28) Invite people to a "lunch and learn" session. Educate them and ask for referrals. "By the way, who else do you think might be in need of my services?"

29) Find a large real estate office. Offer to set up a local art show. Get local galleries to bring art and hang up everywhere. No selling that night. Invite the whole community. Everyone gets exposure to everyone else. Follow up on everyone who attended. Referrals come from follow up.

30) Take clients out for breakfast. Ask them about their lives and business or work. At end ask them how you can improve your service and then ask for referrals.
31) Join real estate organizations, chamber of commerce, BBB, speaker association, service clubs and a yacht club or ski club.
32) Educate your clients all throughout your project that you're looking for referrals. When you get one, send the referrer a 500 minute calling card or some other gift as a surprise thank you gift.
33) Just as you hand a prospect your proposal and they see the price tag say, "I have a special program I'd like to offer you that I don't generally do. If you give me the names of ten people (10 referrals – with names, addresses, phone numbers and email addresses), I will give you a discount of $_____ dollars right now." 99% will take advantage of your offer. Create a bunch of follow up letters to send after you call the referrals. Staying in touch should eventually generate 30-40% more business.
34) After every project ends, send your referrer a thank you note and tell them about the project and enclose a free lottery ticket plus a picture of the before and after.
35) Earn a referral fee yourself by sharing our courses with other people. Say to someone, "This probably isn't for you, but who do you know who might be looking for another career? Who might be dissatisfied in their job or recently laid off? Who might be looking for some part-time income?" Instruct them to give your name and contact information to get VIP treatment. Then we'll send you 10% of the subtotal they purchase. They must mention your name in the notation box below the shipping address in our shopping cart, otherwise we will not be able to credit you with the referral.
36) Get 100% of your personal course fee refunded to you if you refer four other people who each buy one course of equal or greater value to yours.
37) As you get referrals and meet people, you will find many are not ready right then. If you don't stay in touch, they are lost forever. But if you do, you will eventually get a percentage of them to do business with you later. You can stay in touch by sending them a monthly newsletter, by developing a series of follow up letters or postcards that you send out periodically.

Besides having a strong referral generating system in place, you also need to make sure you have an incredibly strong elevator speech prepared – in fact, that you have several speeches you can pull out at the drop of a hat and talk to people about your business. These should be well rehearsed. You should be able to verbalize them instantly – no matter what the situation is – you should never, ever be caught off guard not knowing what to say about your business.

A few weeks ago I happened to meet one of my daughter's friends at a club after her boyfriend's gig. My daughter's friend had just been notified she was to be laid off in two weeks. She was understandably depressed. While we were waiting to leave, I engaged her in conversation about her plans for the immediate future and I specifically asked her, "What are your skill sets?"

After looking at me in shock and stumbling around for words, she finally blurted out that she had "administrative assistant" qualifications. I was not impressed. And when I eventually pulled out of her that she had a degree from a prestigious institution in journalism, I was even less impressed.

This girl had no idea how to articulate anything sensible or valuable about her self to me. Had I been a prospective employer, I would have negated her immediately for consideration. I doubt if she had any idea how she came across to me – someone with the ability to hire people if I chose to do so.

So let's discuss for a minute the elevator speech. What is it? Why is it important?

Why You Need Good Elevator Speeches

You may be asking: What is an elevator speech? An elevator speech is a concise one minute summary that you could give someone to instantly tell them what your business is all about. You should be able to speak this blurb on an elevator going from one floor to another – hence its name. Some elevator speeches can be a little longer or much shorter and you should be prepared with several presentations you can use depending on the circumstances.

Elevator speeches come in very handy when part of a networking group where you have the opportunity in each meeting to stand up and tell others about your business. You never know when an opportunity will present itself where someone asks, "What do you do?" They aren't looking for a long dissertation about you and your services. But they would appreciate an abbreviated blurb that summarizes your business in a nut shell and gives them a good idea about it.

So here are some examples of elevator speeches which you can use verbatim or change as you see fit. The best elevator speeches grab the listener's attention and speak in some manner to the listener that either peaks their curiosity or is filled with strong benefits or that causes them to engage you in further conversation. Good elevator speeches often result in the listener asking for your business card or in generating follow up questions.

By attending social events (parties, gatherings, business meetings, associations), you should have ample opportunities to use your elevator speeches to promote your business. Always have plenty of business cards on hand – and be sure to collect business cards in return. Getting someone's business card is akin to getting their permission to contact them. Yes, you want to give out your card, but it's even more important to get THEIR card and keep the initiative on making further contact to discuss how your services could be beneficial to them or someone they know.

Be sure to change these speeches into words and phrases that make you comfortable. You don't want your elevator speech to differ from your normal pattern of speech (or else it will be "canned" and come across phony). So do take these ideas and reform them into your own style of speech, keeping the essence but not necessarily the style. Sit down and re-write them.

Use these elevator speeches to think up your own. Realize that there is no right way and no wrong way to communicate what you can offer someone. The only way you can fail is to keep your mouth shut and say nothing at all. Missed opportunities create failure and disappointment. So no matter how much time you have, you've got to open your mouth and speak. Start the dialogue. It's easier than you think.

A great way to get someone to ask you what you do is to beat them to the punch by asking them what they do. Most people will return the favor by asking you what you do. It's just common courtesy. So don't neglect to ask. In the Bible it says, "Ask and you shall receive." Speech is free and you should take advantage of all of the opportunities that come your way.

10 Sample Elevator Speeches for Staging or Redesign or Both

HOME STAGING AND REDESIGN

Have you ever heard of the WOW factor in selling a home? Well, that's what I create. I specialize in giving a seller's home that <u>zing</u> that will make it stand out from all the competition – wowing potential buyers with that "special something" which compels them emotionally to decide that this is the home they've been looking for. Using this approach, homes sell more quickly and for the highest possible prices. And for those people staying in their present homes, I generate a new love and appreciation all over again for their home and their furnishings - all in a matter of hours - by rearranging what they already have using professional techniques.

INTERIOR REDESIGN

Have you heard of interior redesign? I specialize in helping people who are bored with their home and with problems they don't know how to solve. I give their home a whole new look by adding just the right amount of sizzle and pizzazz – and in most cases using the furniture and accessories they already have. They are always amazed at how much I accomplish in a matter of hours for a very affordable fee.

HOME STAGING AND REDESIGN

Have you ever bought a new sofa or other major piece of furniture, brought it home only to discover it's too big or you have no clue as to where to put it? Or have you ever looked at a room in your home and realized that it is so full and crowded and overflowing that it looks dreadful? Well, I specialize in taking all your stuff and by using professional design techniques and secrets, turning your room into a charming and inviting space like those rooms you see in decorating magazines. And if you're interested in selling your home, I also specialize in getting your home immaculately ready to sell quickly and for top price. The way you showcase a home on the market is very, very different from how you live in it. So if you're in the market or you know someone else who is in the market, I'm always eager and ready to help. Would you like my business card? And may I have yours?

HOME STAGING

Have you ever decided to buy a specific home only to learn that one or two other people wanted to buy the same home and you'd have to bid against them if you hoped to win out? Have you ever felt the fear that you would lose out on the best home on the market if you didn't submit a bid instantly? This is rough on buyers but great for sellers. Well, I professionally stage homes for my clients and sometimes this creates a bidding frenzy to purchase their home. Do you know anyone currently wanting to sell their home?

HOME STAGING

Selling a home these days requires much more effort than getting it on the multiple listings with an agent. Nowadays you've got to create sizzle – you've got to make a home memorable – you've got to get buyers to fall in love with the property. That's where I come in. With my professional techniques, I know how to give any home a competitive edge against all other homes of comparable size and value. My rates are affordable and I work quickly and efficiently to give more value than any of my competitors. I'm never too busy for referrals, so if you know anyone wanting to sell their home, I'd appreciate a heads up.

HOME STAGING

There's no doubt about it. Selling a home is far more difficult today than ever before – unless you're willing to drop the price by ridiculous amounts. What few homeowners realize is that by using professional home staging techniques, they can avoid the mistakes other owners often make, and they can actually increase the perceived value of their own home for even higher profits. I specialize in analyzing homes, accentuating the assets and diminishing the faults using professional staging techniques and design secrets. My services are very affordable - certainly much lower than the penalty of another price reduction.

HOME STAGING

I help people to stop penalizing themselves by letting their home languish on the market unsold. Isn't it time to regroup and fix what's wrong? As a professional home stager, I specialize in unique techniques and design concepts used successfully across the nation to assist owners in selling their properties for top dollar in extremely short time periods, regardless of market conditions. While I can't guarantee a speedy sale at top dollar, I can guarantee them a far better position and a competitive edge for their home. I work quickly and efficiently at very affordable rates. This is far better than being forced to lower their price and settle for less profit.

INTERIOR REDESIGN

When the economy is strained, smart home owners redecorate and stay put. But few know that redecorating can be instantaneous when using the furniture and accessories they already own. My specialty is using professional techniques and design concepts to turn a home from ho-hum to extraordinary in a matter of hours. I charge an affordable flat fee and my clients are literally amazed at the transformations I have achieved without their having to purchase any new items.

INTERIOR REDESIGN

One of the best values these days is to spruce up a home without purchasing a thing. I specialize in looking at homes and furnishings and then giving an instant makeover in a matter of hours without my clients having to purchase any new items. The client gets to fall in love with their home and their furnishings all over again and finally have the dream home they've always wanted in the process. My services are extremely affordable and I offer a full 100% satisfaction guarantee.

INTERIOR REDESIGN

I help people rearrange their furniture and accessories. I've never seen a room yet that I could not improve. Most people purchase furnishings that work well together – but where they self destruct is in the arrangement. Where they put their stuff is more important than what they have. That's where I come in. I specialize in rearranging what they already have to create the natural beauty of the room and their furnishings, while making the room more functional. I promise them to make a dramatic difference as I reorganize and redistribute their furnishings using professional techniques and secrets. Most rooms are completely done in a matter of hours without having to purchase anything new – all at a very affordable flat rate (or hourly rate).

Ok, now you begin to understand some of our thinking. Now it's time for you to create your own elevator speeches – sound bites – quick and easy talking points that you can use any time, any where, with any one. Look for reasons why your service is valuable. What would you want someone to say to you that would get you excited? If a home stager or a re-designer were to approach you, what would make you hire them?

Write down all the benefits you can think of. Start inserting them into the samples I've given you. Change things around. If a thought seems vague or can't be understood, rewrite it until it is easily understood. Test out your speeches on other people. Note their reactions. If what you say doesn't spawn more curiosity, then work on it until it does.

Ask people for their opinions. Ask people to tell you what would motivate them. Ask people for their ideas. You'd be amazed at what you can glean from just asking questions. Values will differ from one community to another, from one pay scale to another. You need to create your sound bites to fit the type of consumer you are targeting. Share them with me for feedback if you like.

So far we've been dealing with making contact through letters, email, phone and advertisements. But what about your website? What are you communicating on your website, or in a brochure, that could use improvement? In an ever changing business environment that is highly competitive, constantly challenging and where people are inundated constantly by messages coming from the right and the left, you've got to get people's attention instantly. This is no easy task.

30 Attention Getting Headlines

Whether you have a website with a sales letter or you're sending out a letter or postcard, or whether you're writing an article or press release, it is vital to have a great headline. People scan headlines to see if they are interested in reading further and you only have a couple of seconds to grab their attention and garner their interest. So a strong headline is imperative.

Here are some "adapted" headlines taken from some of the most powerful ones ever used. I'm going to first list the actual headline, then give you our adapted headline so you can see how we make applications to our industry. This way you'll not only have some great headlines to test out, but you'll learn how to look at headlines that grab your attention (no matter where you see them) and how to adapt those headlines for your own marketing purposes.

1)   **17,000 blooms from a single plant!**

Adaptation: *5 offers from a single open house!*

2)   **In two seconds, Bayer Aspirin begins to dissolve in your glass.**

Adaptation: In 2 seconds, once simple change made a huge difference.

3)   **Six times white washes.**

Adaptation: Six times more affordable.

4)   **Tastes like you just picked it.**

Adaptation: Looks like you just decorated it.

5)   **At 60 miles per hour, the loudest noise in the Rolls-Royce is the electric clock.**

Adaptation: After 10 clients, the most common complaint is that they didn't find me sooner.

6)   **They laughed when I sat down at the piano – but when I started to play . . .**

Adaptation: They rolled their eyes when I started to move furniture – but when I got done . . .

7)   **Shrinks hemorrhoids without surgery.**

Adaptation: Shrinks time on the market without dropping price.

8)   **9 out of 10 decorators use Wundaweave Carpets for long life at low cost.**

Adaptation: 9 out of 10 homeowners use professional stagers rather than doing the work themselves.

10) **Relieves congestion in all nasal passages instantly.**

Adaptation: Relieves tension over what to discard and how to arrange what you keep.

11) **Here's what you do to get rid of pimples fast.**

Adaptation: Here's what you do to sell your home fast.

12) **Does she or doesn't she? Only her hair dresser knows for sure.**

Adaptation: Does she or doesn't she – only her "home stager" knows for sure. (or insert "decorator" or "redesigner")

13) **Would you believe it? I have a cold!**

Adaptation: Would you believe it? I sold my home!

14) **Floats fat right out of your body.**

Adaptation: Eliminates flaws right out of your house.

15) **What everybody ought to know about the stock and bond business.**

Adaptation: What everybody ought to know about the redesign (or staging) business.

16) **Aunt Mary, who never married . . .**

Adaptation: Aunt Mary, who never sold her home . . .

17) **When you're weary with daytime fatigue, take Alka Seltzer.**

Adaptation: When you're weary with open house fatigue, let us stage your home to sell.

18) **Don't invest one cent of your hard-earned money until you check this guide.**

Adaptation: Don't invest one cent of your hard-earned money until you talk to a home stager.

19)   If you can count to eleven, you can increase your speed and skill at numbers.

Adaptation: If you count on a stager, you can increase your speed in selling and your asking price.

20)   The difference in premium gasoline is in the additives.

Adaptation: The difference in home stagers is in the certification.

21)   See what happens when you crush our executive luggage – nothing.

Adaptation: See what happens when home values crash – nothing.

22)   If you've already taken your vacation, don't read this. It will break your heart.

Adaptation: If you've already put your home on the market, don't read this. It will break your heart.

23)   It took 24 years and genetic engineering to make this product possible.

Adaptation: It took 7 days and a few staging tricks to make this home saleable.

24)   It should be immoral to make money this easily.

Adaptation: It should be immoral to sell a home this easily.

25)   You are twice as smart as you think.

Adaptation: Your home is twice as beautiful as you think.

26)   Now! Chrome plate without heat, electricity, machinery!

Adaptation: Now! A sold home without worry, waiting or reductions!

27)   Who else wants a whiter wash – with no hard work?

Adaptation: Who else wants to sell their home – with no hard work?

28)   Which twin has the Toni? And which has the $15 permanent?

Adaptation: Which home had a professional stager? And which had a 50% price reduction.

29)   To the woman who will settle for nothing less than the presidency of her firm.

Adaptation: To the woman who will settle for nothing less than the full value price for her home.

30)   Melts away ugly fat!

Adaptation: Removes ugly clutter from the home!

So there you have it. Try these out and feel free to rework them any way you like. Be sure and run a test on what you're doing before you commit serious money to it. Next let's explore another great way to drive visitors to your website and interest them in your services or products.

Using Your Vehicle to Promote Your Business

You have the ability to use your vehicle to advertise your business. First, you can have a personalized license plate made through the Department of Motor Vehicles (DMV) in your state. There is a nominal fee each year to keep the personalized plate but if you're lucky enough to get one that is pretty targeted to what you do, it's well worth the added expense. But don't forget you can also have a personalized plate holder or frame made that gives more specifics about your business. It can have your domain name, a tag line, your phone number, a simple email address – whatever you want. As you drive around town on business or personal errands, your message is getting out. You just never know when someone will walk by your vehicle and jot down the information and contact you. How many times have you read the license plates on other vehicles while sitting at a red light? You do the math. It works!

Use one of your adapted headlines on your plate frame or have a magnetic sign made up using your compelling headline along with your contact information. If you stop to think about it, there are many subtle things you can do to spread the word about your business. You never know when someone will read your signage and call you or tell someone else about you. If you're serious about building your business, you want to take advantage of every low cost method you can to promote and advertise it.

Submitting Articles for Publication

Submitting articles to publications and on the web is an excellent way of gaining exposure for your business and using the power of the force multiplier effect. If you have a website and you include a link to it (mind you, only one link per article), you can help build credibility for yourself and get extra page ranking to your website at the same time. By ranking better in the organic search engines, people will be able to find your website more easily.

Articles are different from press releases or sales copy. Study them. See how they are not trying to sell a service or get people to come buy something from the writer. They focus on providing valuable, useable information but they also provide a link back to the author just in case someone wants to make contact or do more research or find out about the author. People respond better when they don't feel they are being "sold" something and they appreciate the free information provided, so long as it has value.

Where to Submit Articles

One easy way to submit blurbs or articles is in my free discussion forum hosted at my website. All you need to do is register with a private username and password, get approved by me or my staff, and post your articles of interest in the appropriate categories. You can even add a link back to your website if you wish. The forum is open to anyone and we have consumers that visit as well as other professionals. As long as your article is informative in a non advertising format, you can have it included quite easily. People will appreciate your contribution and hopefully contact you with a project. It will also help your website gain better rankings in the search engines too. Over time you will also come to be seen as a real professional in the business. As people seek you out for advice they will tell other people who will tell other people and so on.

The URL of the discussion forum is: http://www.decorate-redecorate.com/smf

In addition to my forum, there are other blogs and websites that will accept your contributions. It's a lot of work but, as I've written before, you've got to have several ways you generate business during tough times, not just one or two.

So write informative, helpful articles.

Send them to your local publications. Send them to websites who are open to publishing articles. It takes work, and you have to be patient for results, but it does help you build a strong, sustainable business in the long run.

The Following Article Samples **Not** for Duplication

Following are articles provided to show you examples of the type of articles best suited to get published. They are **NOT free** to be duplicated as that would be an infringement of my copyright. I provide them as EXAMPLES ONLY. Besides, you wouldn't want to post someone's previously posted article as it will do little good for you due to the fact that search engines do not index pages that have been duplicated from other pages already in the index. Search engines like **fresh** content and posting articles that are identical to mine or someone else's articles won't help you very much and it's just not worth making someone angry with you. Just write your own taking ideas from what I've given you and adding your own flavor into the mix.

Notice that each article is roughly 450 words and takes up one page. Do not write articles that are too short; do not write articles that are too long. Do not try to sell anything. Select one key word or phrase and include it in your headline and sprinkle it up to 4 times within the article (if possible). Avoid overuse of the word or phrase as search engines will consider that "spamming" and it will hurt you eventually. Many people try to outsmart the search engines but eventually they get caught and penalized for breaking the rules. Some people have even had their websites kicked off the search engines. So don't try to bypass the rules and "cheat". Work within the guidelines of accepted search engine optimization and in the end you will reap the rewards.

5 REASONS WHY INTERIOR REDESIGN MAKES SUCH A DIFFERENCE

Only a small percentage of homeowners can afford the services of an interior designer. So if someone needs help decorating their home, what can they do without spending a small fortune?

The answers are easy and very affordable according to interior redesign expert and trainer, Barbara Jennings, who is director of the Academy of Staging and Redesign at **Decorate-Redecorate.Com**. "Just about everyone can afford the services of an interior redesigner. The emphasis is on the "re" because most of the time the problem in the home is not what color the wall is or if the furniture "works" - the problem is usually poor placement."

Interior redesign concentrates on placing the furniture and accessories in the proper places, and this is an art unto itself. Unfortunately, this is an area of design that the average homeowner has never learned how to do and most of the time huge improvements can result in a matter of minutes or hours, depending on the situation.

Here are 5 of the most common problems redesigners must address:

1.   **Furniture ignores the room's focal point.** Most rooms have a focal point that is natural or created by the architecture of the home. If there is no natural focal point, one must be created. The seating arrangements should then feature the focal point.

2.   **Furniture is placed too far away.** When furniture arrangements are scattered or placed around the periphery of a room, it often creates "screaming distance" and the room feels awkward and uninviting.

3.   **Scale and proportion are ignored.** The Greeks devised the perfect proportions centuries ago with the Golden Mean Theory. The best ratio is 1:1.6. So when relationships fall well below or well over this proportion, the design loses balance, harmony and beauty.

4.   **Rooms lack unity and flow.** In keeping with the Golden Mean Theory, many homeowners place extremely tall furniture next to low furniture creating a "cliff-like" effect. This is disturbing to the mind and eye. By reducing heights in more gradual increments the visual shock is greatly reduced, thus bringing a rhythmic unity to the room.

5.   **Room lacks sufficient plants and artwork.** Most people do not realize that personality is expressed more precisely through the accessories than by any other element in the home. But it is the accessories that have most often been ignored - particularly in the area of plants and medium to large sized artwork.

By learning how to correctly arrange one's furniture and accessories, it is possible to significantly improve the look and functionality of a room, diminish clutter and make any room more attractive and professional.

4 COLOR TRENDS FOR STAGING A HOME IN _____ (fill in year)

Color trends are constantly changing from year to year. Trends are established at least two years earlier by professional experts from all types of industries who meet and pull together color palettes for consumers. By knowing the upcoming trends, home stagers will keep the home updated and in the best position to be sold.

Here are brief descriptions of the four major trends for 2009:

1) NATURALISTIC TREND The "green" industry has us all focused on using naturalistic products. This means tossing out those that use harmful chemicals or that leave harmful residue behind. This trend preaches the end of the human footprint. The **Naturalistic Trend** encourages pure natural foods, eco-friendly building products, no additives or treatments, everything in its purest form. The softest whites to the darkest grays define this collection. There is only a slight whisper of blue and green. Pure sands of the earth sprinkle tones of beige in this monochromatic trend. Asian themes and styles are perfect blends.

2) WHOLISTIC TREND The **Wholistic Trend** inspires us to live in serene, peaceful spaces while situated in bustling urban areas. Fueled by the wider community it still seeks to reduce pollution and global warming. Instead of sprawling out, the wholistic movement loves organic rooftop gardens. These are particularly useful in metro areas where space is of a premium. A mid-tone palette includes dominant yellow toned greens as well as rich soil brown. It is void of white. Copper and bronze express the earthen elements.

3) NIGHT LIFE TREND The **Night Life Trend** includes stronger colors which fuse with our fast paced lifestyles. These colors feel soothing. It seeks a restful environment that includes our ecological values but also one that respects the balance between earth and its people. All living creatures want to feel secure in their surroundings and we are no different. Green, orange, red and blue is influenced by nightfall. What emerges are deep rich tones that are not bold but serene.

4) INTERNATIONAL TREND The **International Trend** draws from emerging countries. It opens up a wide assortment of individual creativity. Bright colors from around the globe highly influence this trend. Go from mango orange to regal purple and aqua blues to deep lime green. Add those reflective elements of gold and silver to finish off this global trend. Bring in black to share the stage - and even a bit of desert rose.

Best selling author Barbara Jennings, of the Academy of Staging and Redesign hosted at **Decorate-Redecorate.Com** teaches home stagers and interior re-designers how to work with color and other professional techniques so they can help their clients in practical, easy ways.

7 CRITICAL DIFFERENCES BETWEEN POOR HOME STAGERS AND RICH ONES

Studies have shown that there is a major difference between the way people think and feel based on their economic status. These differences are sharply evident in the home staging industry. Here are 5 crucial differences between unsuccessful home staging professionals and successful ones:

1.   Poor stagers look for reasons to fail. Rich stagers look for reasons to succeed. The key is not whether a person fails or succeeds, but how she reacts to both circumstances. Every one fails now and then. The trick is to succeed more than you fail, and to fail in small increments with pre-calculated, measure-able risks.

2.   Poor stagers are jealous of successful stagers. Rich stagers admire other successful stagers. Poor stagers resent others who dress nicely, drive expensive cars, and enjoy the "good life". Rich stagers appreciate the assets of all others, and are not threatened by other entrepreneurs.

3.   Poor stagers believe life is unfair. Rich stagers believe life is what you make of it. Poor people sometimes develop a sense of entitlement, as if the world owes them a free ride. Rich people take pride in earning their own ride and inviting a few friends along for the journey.

4.   Poor stagers concentrate on the obstacles. Rich stagers see obstacles as opportunities. Poor people are afraid they don't know enough to be successful and they want to wait until they feel they know enough before beginning. Rich people know they will never know enough, but they trust they know enough to get started.

5.   Poor stagers focus on the risks. Rich stagers focus on the path. Poor people fear failure so much they don't want to gamble on themselves and would rather keep the status quo than risk the investment of time, effort and money. Rich people believe in themselves, knowing that should they fail, they will regroup and recoup, and wind up even stronger and smarter than before.

Studies have also shown that rich stagers think very differently from poor stagers when it comes to their ability to make money. That's because rich stagers have a very different belief system about wealth that affects not only their thoughts, but their feelings and actions. Consequently the incomes of poor stagers and rich stagers reflect a huge gap when compared, according to Barbara Jennings of **Decorate-Redecorate.Com.**

A person's deep seated subconscious beliefs about money and their worthiness to have it are at the root of why some people are extremely wealthy and other people are extremely poor. Until a person can change their subconscious beliefs about themselves and how they feel about wealth, they will be incapable of changing their income status or their self image.

5 REASONS WHY HOME STAGING SELLS HOMES

It doesn't take a genius to know that the better a home looks the easier it is to sell. Then why do so many people try to sell their homes empty or in deplorable condition? It's not because of lack of time and not always because of lack of funds. So is it lack of common sense or just laziness? (In an "emergency" where the sale must happen quickly, time could be a factor.)

Home staging expert and trainer, Barbara Jennings, is director of the **Academy of Staging and Redesign** hosted at **Decorate-Redecorate.Com**. "I think many people shut down when it comes to preparing their homes for sale. The task feels overwhelming. They have emotionally set their minds and hearts on where they will live next and just don't want to go to the trouble and expense to fix up the home to be sold."

But here are 5 good reasons why every home owner should pay attention to the concept of home staging, whether they hire a professional to stage their home or they do the work themselves.

1.   **Home staging fixes the most glaring negatives in the house.** No one wants to buy a house that looks as if it has been unkempt for many years. No one wants to pay for someone else's mistakes or lack of attention.

2.   **Home staging diminishes the defects in a house.** Every house, no matter how well built, has defects of one kind or another. But even if it were perfect, it will not meet the needs and wants of every potential buyer that sees it. The key is in making sure that the defects are minimized, so it will appeal to the most buyers.

3.   **Home staging actuates the home's attributes.** Every home has a charm all its own but one may have to work at it to bring out that charm. Whether the house is old or relatively new, home staging can go a long way to dramatically enhancing the best features of the house.

4.   **Home staging reaches buyers on an emotional level.** It is a well known fact that buyers do not make offers unless and until they have an emotional connection with a property. But most people struggle with visualizing their furnishings in the home. That's why proper home staging can make a huge statement because it helps them visualize living in the home and even suggests ideas for arrangements.

5.   **Home staging brings the sizzle to the steak.** While some people (mostly men) like seeing the shell of a house, women definitely respond more favorably to a well appointed, nicely decorated home. Once problems are fixed, home staging creates a cozy, comfortable feeling that helps potential buyers make a real, lasting connection.

HOW TO DEVELOP HOME STAGING CLIENTS AMONG THE RICH AND FAMOUS

Most middle class and lower class consumers suffer from a psychological handicap associated with the idea of working with or for wealthy consumers. They can easily be intimidated by people who earn large amounts of money or have well known reputations. If they are in a business that would benefit from dealings with the rich and famous, they shy away because of feelings of insecurity.

Fear of the wealthy shows up in many different ways: when a poor person gives up the right of way to someone driving an expensive vehicle; when there is excessive swooning; when there is stammering, stuttering, name dropping or excessive complimenting when speaking to the rich or famous.

These kinds of reactions are counter productive to being self employed. When in the company of rich people, the timid stop acting normally and start acting unnaturally. This generates a negative response from the wealthy.

In her book titled *Staging Luxurious Homes*, Barbara Jennings (an expert in home staging) suggests that self-employed individuals who are afraid of dealing with wealthy consumers are almost guaranteed to avoid an entire group of people who can truly afford their products and services. This avoidance eliminates the possibility of making substantial profits from a deserving segment of society.

Some of the solutions include tapping into the mindset of upscale homeowners and professionals. If a middle income person learns more about how the rich and famous feel and think, they can overcome those apprehensions. The next hurdle is to learn where to find the rich and famous so they can be approached. There are also certain times of the month and year that are more apt to generate a positive response from the wealthy.

It is a fact that rich and famous people tend to view the world and their part in the world in a completely different way from the average person. This holds true whether they inherited their money or are self-made millionaires. By learning how to find the affluent and how to attract them to one's products and services, by learning how they think, feel and operate, and by knowing when the timing is perfect to approach them, one discovers that they are not to be feared or worshiped. They are to be respected, as are all human beings.

In real estate, when one wants to sell their home, it needs to be presented to the buying public in a professional manner, whether it is a mansion or a shack. Understanding how the rich think is a key ingredient to doing business with them.

For more free tips, visit **Decorate-Redecorate.Com**.

The Power of Leverage

In this guide I'm teaching you about using leverage. When I want to lift a heavy armoire in a client's home, I don't lift it with my hands, arms, shoulders and legs, thereby putting my body (and especially my back) into serious pain or risk personal injury that can last a lifetime.

I use tools that have been keenly developed to help me save my back and body and do most of the work for me. I'm talking about my steel furniture lifter and the carpet and floor sliders I make available to you (see last chapter).

The furniture lifter uses the principle of leverage. I slide it under one leg of the armoire and press down on the other end and it lifts the heavy armoire up enough for me to slide one of the discs under the leg. Then I lift each of the other legs up in the same manner until I have sliders under all four legs of the armoire. Then, no matter how heavy it is or how tall it is, I can easily move the armoire to any place in the room – all by myself.

Leverage takes advantage of other forces to maximize results with minimal effort. So when I submit a carefully crafted article to a website that has a good amount of traffic (visitors) already coming to it, and that web master posts my article on one of their pages, I'm leveraging that website's traffic and it is not costing me one cent to do it.

Let's say that website gets 1000 unique visitors each day. Let's say that 150 of those visitors land on the page that contains my article. That's 150 visitors getting acquainted with me and my website and my services that I did not have to generate for myself. And that page may get 150 visitors (more or less) every day for as long as my article remains on that website.

How great is that?

In addition to that, the back link that I receive from the article helps boost the importance of my own website, helping visitors find my site when they do searches for topics I carry on it.

I tell you, leverage is a wonderful thing. Think about it. How long did that webmaster have to work and how much money did they have to spend to get their website to draw that much traffic? You aren't likely to ever know, but all you need to care about is that you were able to tap into their asset (rank and reputation), and get a direct benefit from doing so without costing you a cent.

Now, what if that site generated 1,000,000 visitors a day? Hmmmmmm.

5-Minute Credibility Booster for Your Material

Want to completely KILL all of the credibility that you've worked so hard to develop with your website? Then I *highly* recommend putting up a site that's FULL of grammar and spelling errors! Just kidding!

Seriously! A couple of spelling mistakes on your website may not *seem* like much of an issue in the overall scheme of things, but to a lot of your visitors, these small errors will be an absolute deal breaker.

That's because many people assume that **the quality of a website's products is only as good as the quality of the site *itself*.**

This is doubly true if you're promoting a newsletter that you wrote *yourself*. Who will feel confident in your skills as a writer if you can't even produce a homepage that's error-free?

Now that's not to say that you have to be a professional writer to write error-free copy. Look at me. I'm not a professional author or copywriter – even though I've written many books, articles and salescopy.

You can still create your own correct copy, regardless of your skill level. Just use your trusty spell checker, plus this **quick guide to the most commonly misused and misspelled words** I've found sometimes in my own copy and on other people's websites.

Commonly misspelled words:

Wrong	Right
alot	a lot
definately	definitely
should of	should have (would have, could have, etc.)
use to (past)	used to
your's	yours

Words that are commonly mixed up:

anecdote	A quick story of something that happened, often used as an illustration of a point.
antidote	A drug that counteracts a poison.
	"He told an anecdote about how they discovered which antidote the patient needed."

complimentary	Free; or saying nice things.

complementary	Related to going well with something else.
	"She was very complimentary about the main course and the complementary side dishes."
everyday	Commonplace, not remarkable.
every day	Two words meaning... well... every 24-hour period.
	"I call it my everyday china, but I eat out so much I don't use it every day."
farther	Describes physical distance.
further	Anything other than physical distance.
	"The farther I traveled from home, the further I came to understand how others live."
home In	To get closer and closer to a target, as in radar.
hone	To polish or perfect.
	"I'm honing my skills at homing in on a niche market."
i.e.,	That is... in other words... what I really mean is...
e.g.,	For example...
X and I	Use "I" when you're performing an action.
X and me	Use "me" when you're the object of the action.
X and myself	Wrong in all circumstances.
	Simple rule: if you eliminated the *"X and"* part of the sentence; which word would you use?
	"The tickets were given to [Jarrod and] me, but [Lisa and] I went to the show."
its	Belonging to it. Possessive, but there's no apostrophe.
it's	It is. This is a contraction, so the apostrophe takes the place of the missing letters and sticks the two words together.
	"It's rumored that the company will lay off half its workforce."
lay, laying, laid	You lay *something* down, you were laying *something* down, you did or have laid *something* down.
lie, lying, lay, lain	You lie down, you were lying down, you lay down in the past, you have lain down.
	"I always have to lie down after I lay tile."
	"He was just lying around when he was supposed to be laying down the rhythm tracks."
	"After the paramedics laid him on the stretcher, he lay there, terrified."
peak	The highest point, the ultimate.
peek	A quick look at something. (So you want to invite people to take a sneak peek, not a sneak peak.)

60

pique	Annoyance (noun); to provoke, invite, or arouse (verb)
	"She took the tram to the peak of the mountain, but due to her fear of heights, was afraid to even peek."
their	Belonging to them.
there	Over there, there is.
	"There's a spot over there where they keep their tools."
whose	Who owns it.
who's	Who is. That contraction thing again.
	Abbott and Costello are the act whose classic bit was "Who's on First."
your	Belonging to you. But almost universally misused in Internet communications to mean...
you're	You are. Again, it's a contraction so it gets an apostrophe.
	"You're about to get a big credibility boost to your site if you fix this one mistake."

A word about apostrophes:

You don't need an apostrophe when you turn a singular noun into a plural.

It doesn't matter what letter the word ends with; it doesn't matter if it's a proper noun; it doesn't matter if it comes from another language; it doesn't matter what part of speech it is when it's not busy being a noun.

Videos *have been replaced by DVDs.*
The Cratchits *had us over for Christmas dinner.*
Petunias *are easy to grow.*
Fastenings *gave way in the storm.*
Porsches *and* Mercedes Benzes *are in demand.*
Opt-ins *signed up in droves.*
The ten-year-olds *hated the clown.*
Cafes *are open for breakfast.*

See? Not an apostrophe in the bunch.

Finally, a note about capitalization:

Avoid capitalizing random words for no particular reason. If it's a proper name of a person, place, or thing, then you can capitalize it. If it's just a regular run-of-the-mill word, don't. If you're in doubt, check the dictionary.

There you go! Just take a few minutes to clean up these very common errors in your copy and you'll put a professional polish on your site.

One last thing – about broken sentences:

You may have noticed that occasionally I use incomplete sentences. This is an author's prerogative. I only do this when I want to make some kind of special emphasis or if I want to be more conversational. After all, this is the say we talk, right? Notice how I just did it on the previous page. Can you find it?

Incomplete sentences are instances where you might want to break the grammatical rules and do a bit of licensing in your writing style. That's ok. Don't over do it.

Additional Tidbits to Test

Through meticulous testing, **some webmasters uncover EXACTLY what's working *right now*,** and decide which techniques aren't worth wasting time trying.

On occasion, I like to pass some of these results along to you to help you make the most of your *own* website. But you must bear in mind that what works today might not work tomorrow so you never just jump into a strategy or tactic and invest huge amounts of time or money to go forward without first testing it yourself. Depending on when you're reading this page, these ideas may still work and might not. I do not guarantee anything because changes happen so rapidly on the internet and one can never be up-to-the-minute accurate.

With that said, **here are a few helpful tips for improving your opt-ins and sales**, courtesy of Senior Internet Marketing Expert/Instructor Cijaye DePradine:

Tip #1: Increase Your Opt-In Rates by Up To 75% with Survey Landing Pages

Want to find out who your market is or find out what they want (and how much they're willing to pay for it)? There's no better way than a survey landing page.

People LOVE to give their opinions on just about anything, particularly if there's a benefit to them for doing it.

But Cijaye recently discovered there's a hidden benefit to doing a survey: she used survey landing pages along with pay-per-click advertising, and was rewarded with **an increase in her opt-in rates of a whopping 75%!** I personally do not recommend pay-per-click advertising unless you have deep pockets and know what you're doing. You can easily lose a lot of money and get poor results. You can also overpay. So be very, very careful if you go down that path.

For those of you who are venturesome, however, the trick is to offer your visitors some kind of "bribe" or reward for filling out the survey, and make sure it's something you can email to them.

Then, at the end of the survey, thank them for participating, and ask for their names and email addresses to send the reward. And presto! **An entire NEW source of opt-ins for your list.**

Of course, the actual results of your survey are just as important as getting the opt-ins, as they'll help you improve your overall business, so make sure you don't just throw up any old thing to get email addresses.

Cijaye finds that her surveys are the most successful when she:

- Makes the pay-per-click ad enticing -- If possible, dangle the free "bribe" in front of your visitors right IN the ad

- Keeps the survey short -- A *maximum* of 10 questions is usually best

- Keep the survey tightly focused -- When writing your questions, concentrate on just one goal. What is the one thing you MOST want to learn from your survey?

Tip #2: Increase Follow-Through on Key Actions with Email Reminders

Is there something in particular you want your subscribers to do? Follow you on Twitter? Join your online forum? Revisit your site to check out new products?

Many people will put a "follow me on Twitter" logo on their website, or place a forum link on their homepage, then just sit back and hope that everyone stumbles across it and decides to follow through.

If that's *your* strategy, you're not going to get very far! In fact, as

Cijaye recently discovered through extensive email testing, by far **the BEST way to get a subscriber to take action is through email reminders**.

And we're not talking the odd email sent once a year. Cijaye says it takes as many as 7 contacts before one of her subscribers takes action!

Okay, we know what you're thinking: If I ask my subscribers to "friend" me on Facebook 7 times in 7 different emails, they're all going to unsubscribe!

But according to Cijaye, your subscribers actually won't mind getting this many email reminders, as long as you follow one very important rule:

ALWAYS answer the "what's in it for me" question!!

So, for instance, if you're trying to get a subscriber to become a friend on Facebook, you'll want to **explain in your emails about all of the *benefits*** of being a friend: They'll have free access to a community of like-minded people they can share ideas with, they'll be able to find out about special offers on your site *before* the general public, and so on.

What subscriber is going to resent you for offering them this kind of help, even if you do it multiple times?

But just to play it safe, you'll also want to pay attention to the *timing* of your email reminders. Send them too close together and chances are you'll see an upswing in un-subscribes.

Tip #3: Increase Purchases and Other Activity on Your Site by Up to 50% by Sending Out Detailed Instructions

Want to get twice as many of your subscribers to take critical action on your site -- like *buy* something?

Cijaye found that simply sending an email with instructions on HOW to act can have a BIG impact!

She sent out detailed instructions for performing a number of different actions on her site, and saw excellent results across the board. Here are some things to try:

- **Leave comments on your blog or site** -- True, getting comments from subscribers won't have a *direct* impact on your sales, but more comments equals more content, which translates to better search rankings, more traffic and *then* more sales.

  Plus, getting comments allows you to create more of a community so that people are more encouraged to come back to your site time and again.

  So Cijaye sent an email to her subscribers, explaining how to leave comments, and voila, **she had an IMMEDIATE increase in the number of subscribers leaving comments**.

- **Join your forum or special gallery** -- Again, getting people *actively* involved in your website creates a community, which leads to repeat visits, and potentially more sales.

  So in an effort to increase the number of people who signed up for her special gallery, Cijaye sent out an email telling people exactly how to do it and **was rewarded with a 50% increase in members!**

- **Purchase more products** -- Believe it or not, you really *can* get people to make more purchases from your website simply by telling them how to do it!

  In this test, Cijaye sent instructions explaining how to purchase products using PayPal and saw an immediate impact on her bottom line.

Why do these three tips we've just shown you work so well? Well, according to Cijaye: "People are simply too busy to figure things out on their own or to remember to take specific actions. It's YOUR job as a business owner to help them along the way... and NOT doing so leaves money on the table!"

Courtesy of MarketingTips.Com

What is a Blog?

At the risk of annoying those of you who already know what a blog is (and may even have an established one of your own), let me briefly explain. Blogs are like personal online diaries that you can start and make entries to every day or whenever you like. Other people can read your blog and, if you allow comments, even place comments on your blog that, hopefully, relate to the entry you made originally.

Blogs are very big and very powerful tools to draw visitors and from your blog redirect them to your website. Every time you make an entry on your blog, it's like placing a new page (albeit a mini page) on the web. And when your readers make comments, these act as new pages as well, increasing the page rank of your blog.

Blog postings are still valuable but they don't have the impact now that they once had because there are just so many of them. But if you enjoy writing and want to add this feature to your business, by all means do so. There are plenty of places where you can start a blog for free. A search on your favorite search engine will produce a number of blog posting sites you can choose from.

The Pink Message Slip Method

Many consultants (and other businesses as well) have found this method of lead generation to be profitable. It's a direct mail method. If you know anything at all about direct mail, you know that the percent of respondents will be small yet you can make some handsome profits if you know how to close the sales and do the proper follow up with the respondents. If you're not good at follow up, however, don't try this method. It has been shown to dramatically increase the percentage of respondents compared to other direct mail methods – which is the only reason I include it here.

I'm sure you've seen the pink post-it pads commonly used by people who have to take messages for other people. Secretaries and administrative assistants use them. You may even use them at your home. Everyone is familiar with them and people pay attention to them because they automatically believe that they have received a phone message from someone and should reply to it.

So right out of the gate you get the recipient to pay close attention to what is on the slip.

Drive around your area and look for houses that are up for sale, or better yet, do your searches online. So many homes are already displaying on various real estate websites and you can even get a peek at the inside to see if it is empty,

66

un-staged or already staged. You won't have the owner's name, but you'll be able to get the agent's name, agent's office address and the address of the property.

Now here is what you do. You handwrite a message that says something like: "Got a call about a possible weakness in your home for sale." Then add your first name only (or your first and last name) and phone number.

Remember, it must be handwritten. Write in fairly large lettering at an angle across the message portion of the slip, as if you were in a hurry. This way it isn't as obvious that you're not filling out the rest of the form. You don't need to have their name or even a date. If you don't want to do the writing yourself, you can have a student, son or daughter with nice penmanship write the notes for you.

Then you stick the pink slip into a nice white envelope and you handwrite the recipient's name and address on the envelope. You can send an envelope that has your return address information on it – or you can even send it in a plain, white envelope with no return address on it. Just make sure the envelope is neat and professional looking and that the recipient's name and address are very legible. Now wait for the phone calls to come in. Again, if you're not comfortable with fielding phone calls, don't do this method. It works best when you simply put a phone number and your first name.

Don't do a huge massive mailing of these until or unless you have first tested its effectiveness. Try different variations. Use different messages. Send them to people who have their homes on the market for sale already if you know they were not staged or if they are empty. Naturally keep good records so that you're not sending this out to the same people repeatedly.

Send them to top selling agents and brokers. Naturally the message would be altered, something like this:

"Got a call that your listing on _____ Avenue may have possible weakness making it less appealing to buyers." Then put your name and phone number.

In direct mail you've got to grab the recipient's attention immediately or your chances of winding up in the trash are huge. I make no promises that it will work for you, but if you never try anything you'll never know. So take this idea and run with it. Come up with ideas of your own.

You could even have your pink slip blown up to the size of a letter for a more humorous slant. As always, be sure to test everything before sending out a large mailing.

Chapter Three
Trading for Services in Tough Times

Why Barter or Trade for Services?

Barter (trading) is the oldest form of doing commerce on the planet. Long before money was invented, barter was the way people transacted business. Unfortunately most people have long ago lost the skill of bartering or trading and aren't even mindful of its power and the ease with which deals can be transacted.

Bartering is particularly valuable to home stagers and re-designers because you are actually paying for what you get with time, effort and expertise – not cash out of your bank account. Ask any entrepreneur who works on a hourly fee if they make money for 100% of their allotted time and they will all tell you it is impossible to sell every hour they have available to invest. Most of the successful ones will only sell 70% of their allotted time, leaving 30% going down the tubes.

Time is something that you can never get back. So if you lose an hour of your time, for which you did not get paid, it is lost forever. On the other hand, time and talent together makes a great product to sell. You do not have any cash expenditures for your time. So whatever you can buy or trade for with time and effort is 100% profit.

When I was an art consultant, I would occasionally barter artwork for some product or service I desired. But I always had costs involved. Yes, I traded at the full retail value of my product and my costs were 50% or less than the retail value, but never-the-less there were costs involved on my end. So I could never barter at a full 100% profit margin unless it was on the installation portion of my services. This meant I was limited on the scope of a trade I could enter and I always had to limit my transactions to what I could afford to pay out in cash for the costs of my products. However, installation was pure labor and time. Since I had to be at the project when the art was delivered anyway, my time and effort to arrange and hang the artwork was valuable and I could value it at a 100% profit margin.

For the interior re-designer, 100% of your gross profit is 100% net profit (minus your real transportation costs). You're merely rearranging someone's furniture and accessories. You don't have any costs for that sale other than your gasoline to get to and from the client's house.

Home staging, on the other hand, can involve some significant costs unless you always structure your deals to leave you out of the loop on aspects where costs are incurred, like in the hiring of sub-contractors for cleaning, repair or replacement, the rental of furniture and so forth.

Trading with Other Companies and Individuals

In good economies, we trade normally in cash. We take what we have (or we feel we can borrow on our credit cards) and that's what we spend. But during tough times, we need to look beyond cash and see what we have of value that can be traded for what we want. Bartering or trading with one's goods or services helps you leverage what you have so you don't leave profits on the plate or table that you could have earned had you had a different mindset. You only have so much cash and you want to conserve as much of it as you can during tough times. You don't want to eat it or have it diminish in value. You can't do anything much about how the government devalues your cash (through inflation and the trashing of the dollar's worth), but you can preserve your cash and use your other assets to gain perhaps even more profits. This is just another part of the force multiplier effect at work.

The first place to start is to make a list of all of the products and services you use on a regular, repetitive basis. Then you match up each product or service to an individual (prospect, client) who could fulfill that for you. In Chapter Five you'll find forms to help you with your lists. Make copies of the generic form and use the copies. This way you'll always have a clean form to make copies from.

For instance, choose either the form for your personal needs or your business needs. One form specifies what you want or need. Another form specifies what your prospects, clients or others need that you might be able to provide. And a third one lists the products or services you have "access" to. Yes, don't restrict your thinking merely to what you can provide – because in a 3-way deal, you can tap into the assets that other people own in order to make a deal happen.

For the purposes of this guide, however, let's focus on creating trade deals you can make that will prosper your business.

Make a list of all the types of companies with whom you will do business on a regular basis or in the near future, either for their products or their services. Use the forms in Chapter Five that are designated for business needs as opposed to personal needs.

Here is a short list to get you going:

Office supply store	Local throw away paper	Carpenters
Gas station	ISP/Domain provider	Plumbers
Accountant	Furniture rental company	Electricians
Tax advisor	Accessory supply stores	Landscapers
Attorney	Furniture stores	House cleaners
Equipment suppliers	Landscaping products	Handyman
Software supplier	Painters	House flippers
Newspaper	Wallpaper hangers	Agents & brokers

Bartering and Trading Ideas

1)   Pick out several convenient home tracts or groups of homes that are convenient to where you work or live. Everyone needs a good home stager at some point or knows someone who does and everyone needs a good re-designer at any point. Barter for whatever asset the homeowner has that you might need now or later in the year. Give them one year to take advantage of your services or allow them to pass your service on to someone else to use. Give them staging "credits" or redesign "credits" that can be applied to your services whenever they are ready. See Barter Scrips in Chapter Five.

2)   Barter your home staging services with local radio or TV stations in exchange for advertising at times that they aren't selling anyway. Give them

staging "credits" to use as listening rewards or to give to their employees or best advertising clients. Do the same thing with redesign "credits". Give the recipients one year to use the credits or lose them. Many will probably go unused and so you got your advertising for free as a result.

3)   Or try a 3-way barter: You provide local hotel with redesign services to freshen up and improve their rooms or staging services for owners or employees - they give un-rented rooms credit which you turn around and barter to local TV or radio station for guests, employees or giveaways - station gives you advertising for your company during their unsold slots. All 3 businesses benefit and no one is out any cash. You give up time you're not being paid for anyway, hotel gives up rooms they can't rent and TV/radio station gives up advertising spots they can sell anyway. Everyone now gets value for assets that would make them no money anyway unless they barter with it.

In tough times the economic climate is perfect for bartering and it can help your business tremendously. These deals must be made with owners or person who pays company's bills to get the most responsive ear and someone with the ability to make the deal.

Segment Your Bartering and Trading Options

Break down the various skills you have learned to develop in your home staging and redesign service. By breaking out the value of smaller portions of a complete service, you will find it easier to fit your services to the value of what the other person brings to the table.

For instance, let's say that you normally charge $3,000 to stage a medium sized home. The service includes the consultation, cleaning, simple repairs, the de-personalizing, the rental of furniture and accessories, the rearrangement of furniture and accessories, some landscaping, and some of the staging tricks to further enhance the property.

You might find it difficult to find a homeowner or agent with ability to barter the whole deal or who sees the value in the whole deal. But let's say they can barter for a portion of the deal. Rather than lose the entire project because you can't figure out how to construct it for both parties, break up the value of what you can give into smaller increments.

Place a value on each of the various components that make up your service. If your prospect can only trade for $1,000 worth of your services, then you can have Scrip just for that portion. Always try to trade on that portion of your service that only involves your time and expertise. You want to avoid having any portion of your part of the deal cost you actual cash.

If you have predetermined the value of each segment of your overall service, it will be super easy to put a portion of the project in the barter status (covered by your Scrip – see Chapter Five) and the rest in cash or just perform a smaller amount of work in exchange for what they have to trade.

If a prospect is still reluctant to do the trade, extend any time limits to use the credits you give out or put no time limits on their ability to redeem them. Remove all risk to seal the deal. Always let the person pass the credits on to other people. After all, if you redeem your credits on the trade, does it really matter who gets the value? The only caution here would be whether the distance between you and the person redeeming the credits is too far to make sense, so you should definitely consider distance when allowing the trade value to be transferable.

For instance, it's one thing to issue credits to someone who lives in your town or city. It is a different matter if they live in a different county or state – or possibly out of the country. So transportation costs or travel costs, that were not part of the original deal must be traded or valued separately or paid in cash at the time the credits are redeemed.

Effective Barter Ads

In order to be successful at bartering, you need to reach as many people as possible. No doubt you will have to educate a certain segment of the population on the benefits and ease of trading with you. In the beginning you may need to advertise. But once you start trading your services for products and services that other people have or other entities have, and you've done an excellent job of honoring your part of the trade, word of mouth will begin to spread and you should find people reaching out to you in time.

So it goes without saying that you should do everything within your power to always honor your part of any trade. You cannot afford to gain a bad reputation. Word spreads like wildfire about people who do not fulfill their promises and that will kill your ability to successfully trade for what you want in the future.

Look it up. There are virtually no categories in the phone book for bartering. But you can go a long way with local shopping newsletters, flyers placed around town, on bulletin boards at grocery stores and at church. People who are already open to the concept of bartering check out bulletin boards. You can even walk neighborhoods leaving your postcards or flyers on doorsteps to spread the word. Take a percentage of the value of each trade you do and put that toward advertising for more projects. In a strained economy, people will love to find out that you are open to bartering, especially if they have bartered in the past or know they have a product or service that has value.

Consider some of the following ideas:

1) Handwritten card placed on a bulletin board
2) A computer generated flyer for local stores and businesses or doorsteps
3) A classified ad in local throw away newspapers
4) A discount coupon in those bulk discount advertising companies
5) Industry publications for real estate or interior design
6) Barter clubs and publications

Before you write an ad or make up a postcard or flyer, first decide:

1) what you have to trade
2) what you want to get for it

You will get the best responses if you are very specific about what you have to trade and its value and very general in describing what you want.

Think about it. Let's say you're willing to stage someone's home in exchange for a week's stay in their vacation home somewhere you and your family will enjoy. Or maybe you need a good reliable transportation vehicle for your daughter going off to college and a home owner has a pre-owned vehicle he has been meaning to put up for sale. Don't specify the make or model in your ad as that will probably be a tough sell. Be open and general and see who responds and what they have to offer.

Now ask yourself these questions:

1) Who will be interested in acquiring your staging services?
2) Who will be interested in acquiring your redesign services?
3) Who is likely to have what you're interested in getting in the trade?

Once you know who is most likely to want what you have, you've got to determine where you need to go to reach them. What publications do they read? Where do they shop? What organizations do they attend?

The most important copy you will write will be the headline. Write a short headline (3-5 words maximum) that grabs their attention. Have it centered over the body copy of the ad. Make it catchy if you can. In the body of the ad you must tell them what you have to offer and what you want in return. Remember, be specific about what you have to offer and be general about what you want in return.

Whenever possible state the value of what you have to give away and the lowest value you are willing to accept. It's a lot more powerful to say: "$5,000 worth of staging services in exchange for $3,000 of _____". Then be sure to put all of your contact information and how and when to reach you. Be sure to put a phone number. You can't possibly say everything you want to say in an ad or even a flyer. But if you get people to call you, you'll be able to fully describe what you have to offer and find out if there is any possibility of a trade right over the phone. There is no sense in wasting either party's time if a deal cannot be made at all.

Don't think that you'll come up with a dynamite ad the first time you write one. There are usually many re-writes. Write down several examples and then set the paper aside for a few days. Come back with fresh eyes and a different outlook and see how you respond to the ads. You'll probably see immediate changes you need to make.

Then have family, friends and neighbors take a look at the ad. Get their reactions. Look for reactions that trigger them wanting to make a phone call. If you can't motivate someone to call you, the ad is a waste of time and money. Of course, ideally you want to barter for the ad in the first place. But that is not always possible. So it behooves you to work hard on the ad copy until you find the best way to state the deal.

Here are some possibilities, but bear in mind, I do not guarantee their success for you. But look at them and see how you can improve on them. Use them at your own discretion.

NEED VACATION RENTAL
Will trade home staging services ($5,000 value)
for one week's use of your vacation property.
Call Mary Jones at 555-1234.

FREE FURNITURE ARRANGEMENT SERVICES
Professional interior re-designer will trade $450 worth of services
for plumbing or electrical services.
Call Mary Jones at 555-1234.

FREE HOME STAGING SERVICES
Professional home stager will trade $5,000 consultation services

for pre-owned vehicle in working condition.
Call Mary Jones at 555-1234.

INTERIOR RE-DESIGN SERVICES TO GIVE AWAY
Certified interior re-designer will rearrange your furnishings
in exchange for beauty products and hair styling.
Call Mary Jones at 555-1234.

You may have to explain your ad to many of the callers. You are not "selling" something – you are offering to "exchange" what you have for what they have. You can give them a period of time in which to use your services and they can even pass the service along to someone else. You can even offer more than one service in the same ad such as:

INTERIOR DESIGN SERVICES FOR FREE
I will prepare your home for sale or make it look spectacular
in exchange for your good condition furniture and accessories
you don't want any more.
Call Mary Jones at 555-1234.

NEED HOME STAGING PROJECTS
Start up home stager needs projects for certification qualifications.
Will stage your home in exchange for unwanted accessories or furniture.
Call Mary Jones at 555-1234.

Do you always have to trade with your home staging and redesign services? Of course not. You can trade using anything of value from your home, your office, your yard, your attic, your other talents and skills. There is no end to what you can offer in trade and no end in what you can accept in trade as well. The only thing holding you back is your need to tap into your own creativity.

You can even take something in trade that you don't want if you feel you can turn around and re-trade it for something you do want. This is a little more risky, of course, but never-the-less a viable way to make a deal.

Bartering for Training

Here is an example of an email request for bartering for one of our courses. It never hurts to inquire. The worst that can happen is that the other party says "no", but then you might get some ideas from that person of how you can still achieve your goal, such as we gave to this aspiring stager.

EMAIL RECEIVED

"Hi, I have over 50,000 miles on US Airways which can also be used with one of their Star Alliance partners. Please let me know if you are interested."

RESPONSE SENT

"We're very sorry but the airline credits would not be enough to barter for a Ruby course. 50,000 miles would only purchase about 1.5 domestic tickets and the value would only be about half of the course's value or less than that.

Perhaps you can barter them with a real estate agent to put up a percentage of the course fee for you. Then if they would purchase the whole course, give them the airline credits plus promise to stage a couple of homes for them after you are trained. Then you have a great practice situation automatically, you get photos for your portfolio immediately, and you're not out a cent. It's good for them and good for you. That way you get the course completely paid for with 'other people's money', not your own."

13 Rules of the Road on Bartering and Trading

1) **Know your market and the values on what you want and need**. If you do not know the value of something being offered to you, do not strike a deal until you've had a chance to research it. The internet is a great resource for you. You can also stock current mail order catalogs for specific types of hard goods items.

2) **Know what your community wants.** This is important because you might see an opportunity to barter for something you don't want or need particularly, but you know someone else does want or need. Some of the more lucrative barters involve several parties, not just two.

3) **Only barter up.** In other words, if you do not feel you will be better off after the trade than before it, do not enter the trade.

4) **Get to know who you are trading with.** Have lunch with people you want to make a significant trade with. Get to know their personality – their ethics – their background. I just signed a contract on a joint venture with a company. My partner and I had lunch with the President and the

Product Development Director before we ever signed on the dotted line. It's important for your trading partner to get to know you too.

5) **Act as if your trading expertise and knowledge is severely limited** (which, in the beginning, it will be). Convey to the other party or parties that they are getting the best of the deal. But remember, only do the trade if you will be better off in the end.

6) **Get the other party to name their price or value first.** Then they are committed to that at the minimum. This leaves you open to counter offer, research, laugh hysterically and so forth. If the other party absolutely refuses to commit first, walk away. If you can't bear to walk away, give them a ridiculously low offer and wait for a counter offer. If there is no counter offer, they weren't serious in the first place.

7) **Never show up for an appointment dressed to kill.** Always dress down so that you are not perceived as rich.

8) **Whenever possible, do a little something nice for the other** party that makes them feel a bit obligated: drive farther, pick up the tab for lunch or a variety of low cost actions. If the other party suggests lunch and pays for it, be sure to send an immediate thank you note.

9) **Time Limits** – In a depression, the value of goods and services go down, making the value of money rise. In inflationary times, the value of goods and services go up, making the purchasing power of money go down. So during normal economic growth or inflationary times, it's wise to put no time limits on when credits you. However, during deflationary times, as goods and services go down in value, it might be wise to put some kind of time limit on when your credits that you issued can be redeemed. During inflationary times, you could conceivably get an extra 1.5 to 2.5% savings on what you trade with because of the eroding purchasing power of the dollar. However, in deflationary times, the opposite is true. Regardless, if time limits must be thrown to the wind, you'll still be able to make a deal that might have failed if time limits were enacted.

10) **Barter only on the retail value (or higher) of the goods and services.** Your actual costs on the products and services you use to barter with will be a good deal less than their cash value. So if your true costs are 50-65% lower than their retail value, your true costs on any trade are substantially lower than if you paid cash. Never ever use your "actual" costs as the basis of the barter.

11) **Always get the goods and services you want up front if possible.** This guarantees you will never be left providing goods and services at a loss. Since you are an ethical person who will always honor your credits (scrip), you'll never have to worry about whether the deal will pan out in the end. This way you'll always be on the receiving end of any discounted value.

12) **By getting the goods and services you want in advance (or up front), you'll in essence become the financier of the trade.** You'll

be able to "pay for" what you get over time at zero interest because you will allow the other party to take a specified amount of time to get the goods and services from you. So this means you don't have to perform your side right away and, as a matter of fact, you might only need to perform your services or deliver your goods a little at a time.

13) **Always insist that the products and services you get will be transferable to a third party**. Naturally you will make deals for goods or services you could use right away. But that won't always be the case. So you'll want the ability to pass the credits or scrip you are holding in reserve on to someone else to use, especially if the other party insists on a time limit to use up their scrip or credits.

Sample Barter Letter

Once you really start thinking about bartering, you'll be amazed at how easily ideas will come to you. For instance, today I was watching TV while having lunch. An advertisement came on from a garage door retailer whom I've seen advertising for years. Because of the economy, he is presently way overstocked, and said so in his ad. He is slashing prices to get rid of inventory.

Now I could take advantage of the lower sales prices and use my cash, or save my cash and leverage my redesign services. I decided to leverage with my talent and keep my cash. I can always use cash if the barter idea doesn't appeal to him.

But if it is a cash deal, his profit on the deal will be drastically below his normal profit margin. Since I will trade him retail value for retail value, he will derive more value in the barter than in a cash deal - and so will I.

I went online and looked up his website. After a couple minutes of roaming around on his site, I found his name, his business address and his personal email address. So I constructed a simple, personal email and sent it off. Here is what I sent him:

Hello _____,

I'm a local interior re-designer and home staging trainer living in Huntington Beach (see http://www.decorate-redecorate.com).

I'm interested in acquiring a new garage door (in black) for my home. I need a door for a two-car garage.

I'd like to trade you at your normal retail value for the door and installation and take away of old garage door in exchange for two full one-day redesign services, which I believe to be of twice the comparable retail value.

I offer half day and full day interior re-design services ($850 value for your area). I work with clients all over Orange County and professionally arrange the furniture and accessories they already own, giving them a finished look equal to what you'd see in House Beautiful. To sweeten the deal, I'll give you 2 days, not just one.

You could use the redesign service for your own home or pass it on to someone else to be used any time in the future. It could be a give away incentive or whatever you wish it to be. I would like to receive the door in the immediate future but will grant you redesign "scrip" which can be redeemed any time in the future you wish to redeem it.

The redesign service is especially valuable for anyone who has a lot of furniture and accessories and is presently unhappy with their home. This fits just about everyone. Since I would be giving two full days, you could use one day for yourself and give or sell the other day to anyone you please.

I believe trading would be very beneficial for both of our companies and will help you reduce your overstock.

Perhaps we could even come up with some additional ideas down the road where we could "partner" since we both serve homeowners but are not competitors in any way.

Please let me know if you are interested.

Warm regards,

Barbara Jennings

Tax Liability When Bartering or Trading

Actually, if you're bartering for a product or service you use in your business and you're giving up your product or service in your industry, you will deduct the value of what you receive against the value of what you give, and there is no tax due. You report it, but the deduction offsets the asset.

And if dealing with a personal trade of goods, so long as the value you receive is less than the original cost or value when purchased, there is no tax liability and you don't even have to report it. (e.g. you trade a used TV for $150 value which originally cost you $500). Trade is less than cost, therefore no tax liability and not even necessary to report.

You barter your home staging or redesign services to the office supply store and get office supplies in return which you use for business purposes and you pick up a new client who will eventually pay you cash for your services, no doubt, unless you're not good at what you do. No tax. If you barter your services for food, however, the value of the food is taxable.

You barter a vacation home you paid $200,000 for trade value of $500,000, then you pay tax on capital gains of $300,000.

So not all barter is taxable nor is all barter even necessary to report. Just depends: yes, no, maybe, sometimes.

Bartering is good business and not just for those who are cash poor either. I once bartered art for dental services for my husband. I'm currently bartering hair products for redesign services. I'm bartering DJ services for a new car. Anything is possible to those with an open mind and creative thinking.

There are many huge corporations who have whole divisions based on bartering and a significant portion of their assets come from sheer barter. Many a company has kept out of bankruptcy, as well, because of their ability to barter.

Using and Developing Your Barter Scrip

Instead of doing business with cash, you can trade with your own "money", commonly called Scrip. It's not illegal. Scrip is merely the same thing as an IOU – a promise to deliver goods or services of a certain value by a certain date. If you've ever used a coupon when purchasing something, you've actually used someone else's scrip. Now you can create your own scrip for other people to use to do business with you.

Scrip should be transferable (just the way cash is transferable). It should state how much it is worth, just as cash states what it is worth. Unlike cash, however, scrip usually has a time limit attached. And unlike cash, scrip must be traded at the full value and not in smaller increments.

For instance, when you purchase an item with cash for $10 and you hand the owner a $20 bill, you would get $10 back in cash. Not so in scrip. In scrip there is no "refund" of a portion of the value of the scrip. Normally if someone is not trading for something at the full value, they would ask for something else to be "thrown into the deal" to make it more equitable. But even then, that is typically done on large transactions, not for small differences in value. Scrip doesn't have to be a coin, like pictured here. It can be anything.

Sample scrip:

Date: _____ Company _____

does hereby agree to permit bearer to redeem this scrip for $<u>value amount</u> (retail price) for any products or services we offer.

This scrip is 100% transferable but must be redeemed by _____ .

No change given if transaction is less than face amount. No refunds or returns allowed.
All items traded on an "as is basis". Sales tax must be paid in cash.

Signature of Authorized Agent of Company _____

If there are any other stipulations you want, you should print them on the scrip as well. But try not to be so restrictive that you deter people from wanting to do business with you.

In Chapter Five I've provided you with some actual Scrip that you can make copies of to use in your trading. There is a Staging Scrip, a Redesign Scrip, as well as an all-purpose Scrip. Feel free to use these forms for your own trading purposes but please remember they are copyrighted and protected and not to be shared with others or sold to others in any manner.

Barter-able Survival Goods in the Worst of Times

In tough times or during localized calamities of epic proportions, bartering can be a life saver and a significant means for protecting your family and putting food on the table. A good example of old fashioned bartering in time of war is the movie, The Pianist. An extremely talented Polish pianist hides in bombed out buildings and his musical talent literally saves him as he is befriended by a German who loves his music and respects his talent. Since no one can predict if they will encounter these types of hard times, it is good to be prepared.

For this reason, I also want to give you this list of some of the products that you'll likely find most popular to barter with and the kinds of products that usually experience great shortages in the stores due to panic buying in emergency situations. Stocking up in advance on these types of products can literally save you, assuming they are not destroyed in some kind of storm, fire, earthquake, flood or major military attack.

Hand soap	Handiwipes	Bags
All purpose cleaner	First Aid kit	Cords
Laundry detergent	Bottled Water	Switches
Rubbing alcohol	Manual can openers	String
Oven cleaner	Fire extinguishers	Rope
Baking soda	Tape (various)	Insect repellent
Dental floss	Thread	Matches
Toilet paper	Liquid detergent	Candles
Seeds	Cleanser	Cloth
Cheesecloth	Disinfectant	Needles
Waterproofing for cloth	Bleach	Yarn
Foot and body oil	Toothpaste	Bobbins
Writing paper	Toothbrushes	Buttons
Pencils	Razor blades	Hooks, Eyes
Erasers	Paper towels	Tailor's chalk
Manual pencil sharpener	Paraffin wax	Wool cards
Glue	Aluminum foil	Dyes
Brooms	Silicone leather seal	Patterns
Mops	Absorbent cotton rags	Zippers
Belts	Pens	Snaps
Appliance repair parts	Pen inks	Sewing awl
Lights	Drafting equipment	Spinning wheel
Tubes	Printer inks	Batting
Household oil	Fax inks	Freeze dried foods
WD40	Steel wool	Gold or silver coins
Portable radio	Scrub brushes	Aspirin or pain relievers
Batteries (all sizes)	Shoelaces	

Note: This is by no means a comprehensive list. Check in survival books or on the internet for more complete information.

Chapter Four
Brokering Deals in Tough Times

Having your own business puts you in the unique situation of being able to broker deals for your own company. You could, if you want, even get involved in brokering deals between other parties – with you being the middle person who makes a percentage of income from both parties that you put together. Sometimes, for some people, it's easier to see deals for other people than it is to see deals for their own company. Either way, you make profit and that's what it's all about, right?

So, particularly in tough times, I don't want you to think solely about doing deals for yourself and your business. At least be open to the idea that you can also make excellent profits coming up with ideas and deals for other people and positioning yourself in between for a share of the profits.

It can be as simple as the following:

1) Select a deal idea for your business or to broker between two or more other parties.
2) Contact the prospects by letter, by email, by phone or in person.
3) Advertise that you are looking for "partners" and get other people to contact you.
4) Educate all parties on the benefits they will receive by entering into the deal. Be sure to stress that everyone wins.
5) Be sure you have researched and done your homework so you're not bringing the wrong parties together.
6) Get all parties involved to sign a Non-Disclosure Agreement. You'll find a sample agreement in Chapter Five.
7) Create and use the appropriate paperwork and documents to pull everything together and make sure everyone participates and earns their appropriate profit. Stay as involved as you need to be to keep control and make things happen – because other parties will usually not be as committed to making things happen as you will be. (Plus your leadership

from the beginning and throughout the entire transaction is the reason you receive a fee.)

As you find and create deals, either for your own business or for other businesses, you're bound to create a reputation. This is very good because you'll start to discover that people will seek you out and you won't have to work as hard to find good deals that will be profitable to you and your clients.

Learning to Think Like a Broker

Generally speaking, you're probably all so tied up in dealing for cash or charging things to your credit card or taking out loans, you tend to have tunnel vision most of the time. It's not your fault. It's a mindset that has been drilled into you since you were a child. You want something – you buy it with cash. You want something that you don't have the cash to purchase – you buy it with a credit card. You want something really expensive (like a home) and you don't have the cash – you buy it with a mortgage.

So you've got to break out of the "cash mindset" and adapt your thinking to a "barter mindset" or "broker mindset". You've got to retrain your brain and your instincts.

Just yesterday my associate mentioned some product or service he felt we needed and should purchase. I looked at him and said, "No, we'll trade for it." Once you've done a deal or two, don't worry, you'll really start thinking differently from then on. You'll be experiencing a paradigm shift in your thought processes. It is important that this transition takes place too, because you're not going to do many deals if you're not thinking like a broker instead of a cash consumer.

What Percentage Should You Get

This is a question everyone asks and wants an answer to and you should know right up front that there are no hard and fast rules for compensation percentages. The really smart and successful brokers work on a performance basis, meaning that they don't earn a cent unless the deal is profitable for their partners. The reason this is so lucrative is that the partners have little to no risk involved and can start and stop any deal whenever they choose to stop. By being willing to assume all or most of the risk yourself, you'll find that deal making becomes many times easier.

With that said, your compensation will depend on a number of factors:

- How much you want or need to make on the deal
- How much your partners are willing to part with
- How fair and equitable you want to be to everyone involved

In most industries, brokers or agents fees are commonly around 10%, except in real estate where the standard percentage or commission is 6%. Of course, 6% of the value of a high priced home can be significant income. When you stop to consider that it takes about the same time to sell a high priced home as a low priced home, you can see that it may be more lucrative to concentrate on higher priced homes.

Since staging is part of the real estate business you may encounter resistance at the 10% level if the parties equate you with a real estate agent. Whenever possible you want to create an individual broker/dealmaker identity that is different from that of an agent – even more important than an agent.

But when you consider that even at 6% from each and every partner you bring together, suddenly 6% becomes 12% (or 18% on a three-way deal). So you need to bear in mind that each deal is different and your compensation could be "standard" or could be very individualized depending on the situation and the parties involved.

When you consider that you could broker a hundred deals per year or more, the income potential starts to become staggering. Let's say your deal comes to $50,000 total profit. A 10% commission would be $5000 and a 6% commission would be $3000. Do one hundred deals in 365 days and you've just earned $500,000 for the year or $300,000 for the year. Either way you will have earned more money than the average attorney.

But let's say a deal comes along where you can get 40% of the profit. On a $50,000 deal, that would net out to a neat $20,000 just for that deal alone. Pretty cool. Would you say that would fix whatever financial problems you're having? Would you say that would grow your home staging business exponentially?

Did I also mention this can all be done with a phone and a computer on your dining room table?

I know what you're thinking. You're thinking – yeah, that's great and I love the idea but I can't seem to think of any deals. Help me.

I know what you're feeling. Believe me, I've been there myself. But here is where you're going to have to cut the umbilical cord and venture out on your own. But never fear. The extensive forms I've created in the next chapter are really going to help you generate ideas for deals because, if you fill out the forms and give the proper time and respect to thinking and writing things down, you will find that the ideas just begin to come.

There is no secret that you can grab from the outside. You've got to look inward. The ideas and the contacts you already have. You'll find them but only if you do the homework and fill out the forms.

Under-Utilized Assets of Others

Every business you encounter out there, whether doing well or not doing so well, has assets that have been under-utilized. These assets have value but the owner usually doesn't realize the true value of their assets. One of the most overlooked assets a business has is its list of present and former customers. When people do business with a company, they do so because they have a measure of confidence and trust in that company. If the experience is a good one, they will prefer to transact business with that same company again rather than finding another company instead.

So in any given business out there, the former customers and present customers or clients have a definite value. The greater effort that has been expended building a relationship over time with those customers or clients, the more value that list has. If the owner of the list has been careful and protective of the people on his/her list, they will tend to trust that owner and take suggestions from that owner.

You, as a home stager, have the ability to take advantage of that trust and take advantage of all the years and dollars that have been invested into building that list of present and former customers. However, <u>never share the specifics of your proposal until you have a signed confidentiality agreement with the businesses you have selected</u>. There is a sample agreement later in this guide. You want to make sure you have a signed agreement of profit splitting before ever divulging your concepts to anyone.

So now here's how you do it.

First you must understand that no matter what type of business it is, the people that transact or transacted with the company also buy other products and services they want and need which may be directly related to that business or completely unrelated. I mean, every person in the world needs groceries and clothing. Most of these people also need insurance, banking services, automobiles, accounting services and so forth.

If you were to go to any company out there with a mailing list or email list of their present and former customers or clients and get the owner of the list to write to their list and recommend your services should they ever need anyone to help them sell their home (or the home of anyone they are related to or know), the response rate will be many, many times higher than if you were to contact them yourself.

If you contacted them it would be a "cold" contact. But if the list owner contacts them and recommends you to them, it is a "warm" contact. This is what is known as a 3rd party endorsement and it rarely gets any better than that. Naturally any business that you would derive from the endorsement would need to be split with the owner of the list, but it would be well worth doing, even if your profit on the initial project is less than if you generated the client on your own.

Not only do you stand to gain new clients from the mailing, but you'll also have the chance to pick up all of the referrals those clients can give you once you do an outstanding job for them.

Can you think of a better way to take advantage of the assets that belong to other people and do so without it costing you one cent on the front end? Do you think this type of mailing would generate more profits than if you purchase a cold mailing list from a mailing list house? Absolutely!

One of the additional benefits is that you will be helping the list owner take better an advantage of his own asset than before. A successful mailing will or should open his/her eyes to the goldmine of his or her proprietary list.

And when you are successful in generating more clients from this list, you can repeat this endorsement idea all over town with countless numbers of other businesses who have their own unique mailing lists.

What if (by way of example) the business you first contacted was a real estate appraisal company. Let's say they have a list of present and past clients whose homes they had appraised. What if they wrote a personal letter sort of like this one on their company letterhead:

Dear Friends:

Last week my wife and I were driving through the area and couldn't help but notice the growing number of bank owned houses with signs on the front yard. We also noticed an increase in homes we know are being sold short. It was disheartening to be sure.

Since our company anniversary is around the corner, we couldn't help but be grateful that business has continued to be good to us, and we felt compelled to express our heart felt feelings and appreciation to you as a client. After all, if it were not for clients like you, we might find ourselves in the same predicament as so many others in the neighborhood.

So we decided it was time to say thank you to you in a unique and different way – not with a store bought card – but with actions, not words.

Let me explain.

A friend of ours is a local home stager, who has built an incredible reputation in her industry as a caring consultant who works extremely hard on behalf of her clients. I have always known her to put the needs of her clients well above her own. We were talking recently and I explained how I wanted to do something very special for my friends and clients that would express my gratitude for their business. I further explained to her how I wanted to do something that would really benefit them or anyone they knew and at the same time express my thanks with ACTIONS rather than WORDS in a card.

After a bit of "arm twisting", she agreed to allow my clients who call her and mention this letter in the next 30 days to receive a 20% discount for her consulting which can be used any time within the next 12 months. Since she would be providing you and your friends with the finest consulting service in the industry to help you maximize the profits from any home you want to sell, she believes you will continue to recommend her services to others. So she agreed.

So feel free to call her any time in the next 30 days at XXX XXX-XXXX and mention this letter so that you'll lock in that discount for the next 12 months. You'll also receive her VIP treatment as well as her appreciation to me for sending you this letter.

Since none of us know what the future of real estate values will be in the coming months and years, and since home staging is one of the absolute best strategies to use when selling a home, we felt this would be a much better way to show our gratitude than sending you a card.

All of our best wishes,

John and Mary Doe, XYZ Appraisers

Play around with your letters. Make it "their" letter. It should be written just like they speak – so forget about grammar, syntax and the like – let them just speak the truth and talk to their people like they would want to be talked to. An honest approach – a truthful approach – will go a long way in getting the audience to respond favorably.

Please recognize that this type of approach is good both for the appraiser and for you and for the recipients of the mailing. The appraiser has done something unique and very valuable for his entire list and anyone else they share the letter with. He has also proven that he has their best interests at heart and that he is a grateful person. This is good for his business and will probably generate repeat business for him as well as generate new business for you.

It is important when contacting any company to write an endorsement for you that you explain the intrinsic value of their list to them and the lifetime value of their customers. So often businesses fail to think of their clients and customers as bringing them value over a lifetime and only think of them as valuable in the short term. All too often they never contact them again – they never contact them repeatedly in well timed communications. They never think of bringing them something of value as a way of saying thanks. If they do send out their thanks, they usually send a postcard or a greeting card. That's nice, but what benefit does it really have for the recipient? Not much.

Tying the Letter to a Reason

These types of letters are best sent out with a reason given in the letter that makes it justifiable. In the example above, the reason was pure gratitude for having a growing business and an upcoming company anniversary. But there are many other reasons one could use to justify sending out a letter:

- We've just discovered the most incredible . . .
- We've learned of a secret method . . .
- Since my friend is just starting off her business . . .
- This is the most incredible way for you to . . .
- It's only fair we tell you before the rest of the community learns . . .
- We felt we would be remiss if we didn't get you in touch with . . .
- Christmas is fast approaching and we wanted to say more than . . .
- We're about to go on vacation, but before we leave . . .
- Home values continue to drop so we felt it imperative . . .
- A friend of mine just went into foreclosure so . . .
- Of all the houses I listed last year, I thought you should know . . .
- I read in the paper this week . . .
- My daughter bought her first home last month and I got to thinking . . .

You get the idea I'm sure.

It's important for all parties to know that not everyone will respond. However, a certain percentage of them will respond. Even if you wind up making far less on each consultation you give, you will be advancing your business dramatically in ways you could not have done on your own. The referrals alone make the deal worthwhile, even if your initial profit is very, very low. And once you have successfully helped these respondents, they will probably use your services over and over again in the future – not at the discounted rate – but at your regular rate.

So now that you understand how lucrative this approach can be for your business (and all parties), I know you're wondering how you should go about approaching the businesses in your area with your "pitch". Here's how.

You can write them, call them or drop into their establishment. Then you convey the following message:

> "If I show you how to properly utilize an asset you are overlooking and make you look like a 'knight in shining armor', would you be willing to take a look at my idea? It can earn you new-found profits and generate immense goodwill at the same time."

You can structure it thusly:

- The letter should generate new business for the list owner, from which you get 50% of the profit
- The letter should generate new business for you, the stager, from which the list owner makes 50% profit
- Both of you are bound to generate new referrals and new clients which can be a profit sharing agreement or not, as you choose

There are no rules and you can structure the deal any way you wish. A simple explanation combined with a written document should easily convince any business owner of the validity and value of doing such a deal with you.

One last thing. When selecting companies to endorse you, it will probably be far more lucrative if the business is related to home ownership in some way. We are fortunate to be in a business that has a commodity that most people own, regardless of who they are, where they live, what business they are in, or what products and services they purchase. So an endorsement can be good no matter what type of business it is, but it will probably be more valuable and the response will probably be higher if there is a real connection of some sort.

If you want to do a few "practice" deals first, select non related industries and then when you have it polished, approach the more related industries.

In conclusion, I hope you can see that this is an often overlooked and practically untapped area of marketing. You have the ability to cash in on other people's lack of observation or understanding of the lifetime value of their own clients or customers. You'll be doing a noble service that will be a win/win for everyone involved. And if you really like setting up these kinds of deals for your business, you might one day start setting up deals for other companies and, for instance, marry car dealers with detail shops. You could introduce dental patients to companies who sell teeth whitener. You could introduce yard maintenance people to tree trimmers and so on and so on and so on. The list is endless and you simply put yourself in the middle of each deal to make a small profit from all the companies involved. They do all the work once the deal is set up and you just bank your profits. Sweet.

Farming Your Community

For decades real estate agents have routinely sent out mailings to home owners in their community to keep their names before the public. In the real estate market it is referred to as "farming" a community. I can remember the days when I would get flyers, brochures, note pads, refrigerator magnets and a host of other things either mailed to me or dropped off on my doorstep. It obviously paid off for the agents or they would have stopped doing it.

Now it is less common to receive promotional materials at my door – probably because of the internet and the fact that many people shop for agents and homes on their own over the web. However, farming still has a positive effect and because so few agents promote themselves in this manner any more, the <u>competition</u> to attract the homeowner's attention is practically non-existent.

So why not contact the top agents in your area who are still using offline techniques and offer to do a joint mailing or joint drop off with them. Get them to restructure their message to include you and your business as an additional benefit the owner will get by listing with them. By joining forces, you can increase the potential response from recipients and you cut the costs in half for both of you.

To make your message stronger, contact agents out of your area and request they mail you whatever they mail out. If need be, you can buy or have your agent buy the rights to use their letters, postcards or mail-outs, with your contact information of course. If you don't buy the rights, you could kick back a percentage of the profits to them for being able to use their marketing strategies <u>out of their area</u> so you are not competitive in any way. Study the strengths and weaknesses of what you get back and incorporate the good parts into your mailings and avoid anything you see in their mailings that was not effective.

Focus the message on how the consumer (homeowner) will benefit and how hard you will work to earn their respect and referrals once you have completed your assignment. You'll also need to check to make sure you can do a joint mailing without having a real estate license. Don't violate the law.

If you can legally do this kind of joint marketing, the added benefits of a fuller service can be just enough to dramatically increase the responses.

Point of Purchase Displays

We've all been to a number of restaurants that put "tent cards" or cards on display stands on the table or the counter that tantalize the patron to purchase that particular item, not only by the fabulous picture that shows the item but by the captions that go with the photos.

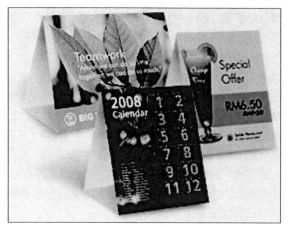

For instance, picture a piece of peach pie and a cup of steaming hot coffee with the caption, "hot, moist peach pie, made fresh today with locally grown peaches, served with freshly whipped cream and piping hot, fresh coffee". Could you resist? Even though I don't drink coffee, it would definitely be a temptation for me.

National chain fast food restaurants have discovered a marketing tactic that brings in tons of additional sales for the advertised products on these cards. And as amazingly successful as this idea is, there is a huge segment of that industry that never use this powerful marketing strategy.

I'm not advocating that you contact restaurants, but you can learn a lot from other industries about what to do in your own industry. You've just got to think about how you adapt the idea over to the staging industry.

So what do you think would happen for your business if you took some of your best before and after pictures and printed them on a tent card. You could have the before picture on one side and the after picture on the other side. Or you could put the pictures side by side on the front of the tent card and your contact information on the reverse side.

You visit real estate agents and merely ask to have your tent cards placed in their lobby and in their offices. You promise them a percentage of every project you get as a result of the tent cards. With this method you will be leveraging their in-house visitors. Not only will their clients see that staging services are available to them, you will be viewed as a separate entity that the agent endorses as professional.

It costs the agency nothing to have you place your tent card or display card in their office and they make passive, residual income from all profits you generate thereby. It's a win-win for everyone – most especially for the sellers who visit their offices.

One such company that makes tent cards is ExCard.Com, but you can also search on the internet for competitors to find the best deal for you.

Naturally you don't need to keep this idea exclusively for real estate agents. You can literally place these cards anywhere you are allowed to. Even though the industry might be different from real estate, the beauty is that home owners are everywhere and doing business with every conceivable type of industry out there, so every person who owns a house is your target market. One day everyone needs or wants to sell their home.

As for the type of text you would put with your fabulous before and after photos, try to make it tantalizing and benefit driven. Here are some examples:

"Sharon didn't believe home staging would really help her sell her house . . . until she got an extra $10,000 offer in less than 2 weeks."

"You only get a few seconds to make a great first impression! After that, the opportunity is lost forever. Don't lose out! Professional home staging services that entice buyers left and right."

"Home staging that is fresh, exciting and individual – brought to your home in a single day and backed by our 100% satisfaction guarantee."

"Home staging that sizzles your home like a hot steak on the grill. Mouth watering design techniques that make buyers order up an offer that can't be refused."

The great thing about these tent cards is that they aren't that hard to have made or to change as needed. Every time your staged home sells, you could mention how much extra profit you helped the owner make and how fast it sold on the market. You could supply an on-going, ever changing group of photos, particularly if they represent homes that the agency listed.

Before you present your idea to an agency, be sure to get a signed non-disclosure contract with them, so that you are protected should they decide to make up their own tent cards. This is a great way to generate sales and you want to have a percentage of the extra profits the other company makes, whether the tent card advertises your staging services or whether the agency advertises their sold listings that don't involve you. As always, before you roll out a large campaign with many establishments, always do a test to make sure your card has a winning message.

Licensing Rights from the Successful

Let's say you're either relatively new to home staging or you've been floundering around trying to find a winning way to build your clientele. Everything you've tried has proven to be ineffective or you don't have the resources to try and test one idea against another one. Therefore you're very hesitant to try anything at all that requires an investment of any kind.

Happily you don't have to reinvent the wheel, so to speak. All you have to do is look for highly successful stagers in other parts of the country who are not your direct competitors. You contact them and see how business is going. You offer to buy the rights to use their marketing materials, tactics and strategies in your area of the country, assuring them that you will never be their competitor.

By licensing the rights to use (and then adapt) their proven methods, you can build your own clientele in your community with materials and tactics that have already worked for someone else. So there's little to no guess work.

Not everyone will be open to the idea. But some will. You sign an agreement with them to pay them a percentage of every new project you get from then on. It's the perfect passive income for them and a winner for you too.

Leveraging Customer Lists of Bankrupt Companies

Contact the attorneys in your area and ask them if they are handling the bankruptcy proceedings for any home staging or real estate companies. Attorneys generally do not think about the real value of the customer or client lists of companies going out of business. But these lists have value.

There will be a percentage of clients that got burned by the bankrupt company but you'll find that the majority were probably serviced nicely and were satisfied. You can then use the lists any way you want. You can solicit the names on the list yourself. You can use them to barter for services or for something you want to do with a competing real estate agency. Or you can resell the rights to the bankruptcy company's competitors and still use the list for your own purposes, so long as they are not competitive.

You can also watch the legal notices of your local newspapers where companies that are filing for bankruptcy are listed. Make bids for the exclusive or non-exclusive use of their active customers, prospects and client lists. You could even try to get the use of the company's name and logo to use as an endorsement for your company.

E.g. "ABC Real Estate has unfortunately been forced to file for bankruptcy but would like you to know that XYZ Home Staging is their pick for staging your home for sale. (XYZ Home Staging is not affiliated with ABC Real Estate.)"

I wouldn't offer cash for access to these bankrupt assets. I would offer payment on a contingency basis. Then you don't have to pay for the asset unless or until the asset you acquired rights on has produced profits for you. If you sell the list, you give a portion of the profits to the bankrupt company's owner. If you get projects from the list, you give a percentage of the profit to the owner as well. You're helping the owner who is suffering a loss to make some passive income from assets he/she spent money developing and you're leveraging all of that for your own profit, which could benefit you for years to come.

Here are some other ways you can track down companies facing bankruptcy or who have already gone out of business. Ideally you want to find them before they get to the point where attorneys and courts must approve any transaction:

1) You get lists of bankrupt companies from public records.
2) You talk to vendors or suppliers and get lists of companies in serious non-performance of agreements or paying for products they ordered.
3) You get lists of companies in financial trouble from commercial loan brokers.
4) You check out your local legal notices in newspapers and online.

What if you stumbled across a company about to go out of business who had a customer/client list of 150,000 names? Do you think you could find a way to profit by mailing to or contacting all those names? How long would it take you? Do you think you could peddle that list for a price to that company's competitors for a profit? I bet you could.

Liquidating Assets – Your Goldmine

In tough times many companies don't survive. Even in good times, many companies do not survive. In addition to survival, almost all companies develop assets that they don't fully utilize. I myself recognize I have many assets I've totally ignored or don't have time to monetize or maximize. So there is opportunity all around you if you will look for it.

Periodically I get an email from someone in the industry who has props of all sorts that they want to liquidate because they're getting out of the business for one reason or another. But they aren't the only ones who have assets they need to monetize, maximize or discard.

Every retailer and wholesaler winds up with products that are perfectly good but which for various reasons are no longer selling or that have never sold that well. They would just love to get rid of them – even if they have to take a loss.

You can gain all of those savings by picking up their un-saleable inventory or overstocked inventory. Heck, this is what Overstock.Com has made a fortune doing. Many retailers have product on their shelves that was someone else's over-runs or discontinued items or seconds. When you buy or trade for this type of merchandise you're leveraging your assets to the max.

Just yesterday I received the following email from one of my Diamond students:

"By the way, I've taken the advice about Garage Sale Organizer from one of your books and I've booked two yard sales already. One is a huge antique sale, at client's building! Beautiful antiques. I've got a signed contract and a waiver of liability from this one. (thanks to some of your samples). I'm charging $200 prep fee and 25% of all sales. I can't wait. . . . Also got another one for this weekend. Having it at my home. Clients don't want stuff back, and it took 3 trucks to bring it all. I have found MANY treasures going through their stuff. Steubenville China, Goebel Figurines, Crown Castle ltd dinnerware, etc. Only one week of an ad in my local paper and flyers around town brought those two sales. So far so good! Couldn't have done it without your great guidance and ideas! Hopefully it's the start of my business I've named Wright at Home Interior Solutions. – Kim Wright (Wright at Home Interior Solutions". At this writing she doesn't have a website yet, but you can see if there is one there at the time you're reading this : www.wrightathomeinteriors.com.

UPDATE FROM KIM
"My ad for the sale organizing goes something like this:

Need to have a yard sale but don't want the hassle? Let a professional do it for you. I will plan, pack, inventory, advertise, price, and SELL your unwanted treasures. Your location or mine. Easy Money! 25+ years experience w/ great references. Please call to schedule your sale today.

"I landed a large sale of antiques in an old store the client owns - full of treasures. I'm charging $25/hr for prep work - I estimate to be about 8 hours - client pays for advertising (I get a discount because I work for the newspapers), then I'm charging 25% of sales.

"Last weekend I had a client who just wanted to get rid of their stuff. Already boxed, labeled, etc. I charged $25 for pick up and 50% of sales to store stuff and sell at my discretion.

"I've worked out a deal with my employer to have a monthly sale at the newspaper which is in a great location in town. I will bring quality stuff from clients to this monthly sale. Client continues to make money throughout the season - as do I. Also, I'm running across a lot of accessories I can use in staging & redesign. I've had great response to the ad I put in paper, people saying what a great idea, great service, etc. I've put flyers up around town and pass out my business cards whenever I get the chance.   It's not something I want to focus my business on, but sure helps get references, contacts, make some money etc., until I get total certification and staging letters out. At sale, I also set up a table tent with my business info and cards to give to people."

You see what can happen when you take one of the ideas I throw out there and run with it. Kim is doing just that and I have no doubt she will go on to become very successful in her business. She's not afraid to try things and put forth the action to make it happen. All too often people read but don't act. You've got to jump on the ideas and make them work for you. Rewards are out there waiting for those that do.

Leveraging Under-Utilized Space

Most home stagers work from their home but some open up offices. To pay for an office all by yourself seems rather foolish, in my opinion, because you really don't have to go down that path unless you want to do so. Please know that it is very customary to work from your home. But should you decide you prefer a commercial address, why not approach some business that has extra unused space and co-opt with them for the space? You'll save a good deal of money in the process and they will benefit as well.

But that's not the only way to take advantage of another company's extra space. Look around your immediate area for retail or wholesale space that other people have where there is extra space. You could put up a display in their space. You could use counter space. You could use window space. You could set up a vignette with signs about your services.

You could gather a group of related business where none compete with each other and co-opt space together in a host company's under-utilized offices, lobby or warehouse. My husband operates a company that is totally unrelated to my company and he has a large warehouse. Guess who uses his un-used space?

You'll probably need to be added to their liability insurance policy or carry one of your own. But this is a great way to have storage for your props without paying through the nose for space or maxing out your garage.

Leveraging Under-Utilized Personnel

What would happen if you found a company that had a whole network of telephone solicitors and they only paid their people for the day shift? What if you approached them with a small staff of personnel to use their facilities during the hours the facility is empty? Perhaps they would provide the staff at a reduced rate during the "off hours". In tough times most companies quickly recognize areas of their business that are not being used to full capacity and so making special deals with them at a reduced rate or on a contingency basis has an appeal to them and it can really help you build your business without you having to do all the promotions yourself.

Take moving companies. Contact them about using their trucks or personnel during "off hours" for your clients at a reduced rate or in trade for something. When I pass by my local "rent-a-van" company, its amazing to me how many hours per day their trucks are just sitting on their lot not being used. With the right approach you should be able to contract with them for savings that you can pocket or pass on to your clients.

Almost every company out there has raw materials they no longer need, finished goods they no longer can sell or need, capacity they aren't fully utilizing, personnel sitting around doing nothing and so on. During tough times these issues are magnified more than usual. As a smart marketer of home staging services, you can take advantage of these issues in a way that will help the companies you deal with stay in business and help yourself and your own clients out in very big, meaningful ways.

Leveraging Security Breaches

Years ago when my children were in grade school I partnered with an art company about 15 minutes away to run their corporate art division. So when my children were at school, I worked at the gallery. My plan was to come home every day by the time they got home from school, but as time went on I found myself staying at the office longer.

When my son and daughter got home from school each day (school was 2 blocks away), they would phone me that they were home safely. One day I got a call from my son who was in great distress. They had come home to an open door and my home had been ransacked by a thief. All of my larger furnishings were still there, but money, jewelry and small electronics had been stolen. I told my son to take his sister and go next door immediately and wait for me and to have the neighbor call 911.

I raced home not knowing whether the thief was still on the premises or not. Fortunately he was long gone. I lost about $7000 worth of possessions. But more than that, I decided it was the last day I would ever allow my children to come home to an empty house. We all felt violated - emotionally, mentally and physically.

While no one would wish such an experience on anyone else, there are people who have their homes ransacked who never get over the experience and no longer wish to continue to live in the home. A well-timed promotional piece offering to help them prepare their home for at a discounted price would be a good way to help someone going through their difficult aftermath.

Watch your local TV and newspapers for alerts about such events. You can also sign up to receive monthly newsletters from your local Neighborhood Watch organizations and by becoming actively involved you'll learn who in the community has experienced an unfortunate incident that might now want to sell a home.

Perhaps you could even broker a deal with some of the security monitoring services whereby you get alerted when they have had to call the police about a break in. You would pay them a percentage of your profits if a customer hires you to stage their home.

Using Your Vendors As Leverage With Their Full Permission and Gratitude

I hope by now you've also caught on to the fact that your vendors – the people who need you to be successful so they can be successful – are a great source of new business potential for you. They probably serve a similar demographic and a similar customer or client to yours. The types of vendors mentioned in this chapter are particularly good for you because they are in and out of people's homes all the time. They know who is new to the area. They know who is thinking of selling their home. They know when a house gets listed.

99

They may know the agents personally. Even if they don't know the agent, they know when the "for sale" sign goes up and can put you in touch right away with the agent of record.

Recognize that your vendors have a vested interest in seeing you become more successful, because as you grow your business, you're likely to automatically help them grow their business too. That makes them the perfect candidates to feed you with referrals or insider information that would be difficult or near impossible for you to ferret out on your own. It also makes them perfect candidates to send out an endorsement letter on your behalf to their customer list, as discussed earlier.

So make sure you establish a healthy, warm, congenial two-way relationship with all the product providers or service providers that you intend to do business with regularly. Let them know that you expect to get referrals from them. Let them know you expect to get advance knowledge of changes in the marketplace.

They can be a serious source of valuable information for you and put you way ahead of the competition in your area as a result. See Chapter Six for how to hire vendors to meet your client's staging needs.

Leveraging Co-Opt Advertising

Why fund all your advertising yourself? Did you know there are many companies out there, particularly vendors and suppliers, who are more than willing to contribute money to help you advertise their product or service along with your own? Any company that would benefit by your success is a target for co-opt advertising deals. I've already mentioned approaching a real estate agency to add you to their marketing where you'll pay for a portion of their costs or where you'll trade your services for being added to their current advertising.

But you can turn that around and plan out your own advertising campaigns and enlist co-opt dollars from your suppliers and others to help you pay for your campaign. Let's see what types of companies may have co-opt dollars just waiting for you to request: moving companies, contractors, plumbers, electricians, hardware companies, carpet companies, landscapers, furniture rental companies and so forth.

They aren't thinking about helping you build your business so you've got to approach them instead. But when approached correctly, you may find many of them will match you dollar for dollar and that cuts your expenditures in half.

Naturally one of the best ways to leverage the cooperation of vendors and suppliers (and anyone else for that matter) is to get them to endorse you and your services to their online base of customers and prospects. A well timed email or newsletter can generate hundreds or thousands of dollars in profit for you. An article, blurb or ad on their highly visited website can generate business for you too. Even my own website hosts a directory by state and city which you should make sure you are listed in.

So there are many, many different ways to build your business. The more creatively you think and operate, the more money you will save, the more progress you will make and all this together will help you build your business in tough times as well as good times.

Utilizing the Home Staging "Mark-Down" Bandit

Pay a visit to your local hardware store manager. Explain your services to him or her. Tell the manager you'd like to be their "home staging mark-down bandit" who shows up once or twice a month (sort of like the K-Mart blue light special). The blue light special has been used very effectively by K-Mart to announce special sales in certain departments of the store for a limited time period (15 minutes, one hour, 2 hours, Friday only and so forth). I've been in stores when the blue light special came around and a throng of people would always come quickly or even follow the blue light around the store to see where it went next. The blue light special always attracts interested buyers already shopping in the store and the fact that the special is for a limited time only, it entices people to buy things they might not ordinarily buy.

You can do the same concept with the home staging markdown bandit. You could dress up like a bandit or have someone else do it for you. I mean, who could resist a bandit that looks like this? Remember hardware stores are heavily frequented by men. If you don't want to be a bandit, be anything you want – even a pirate or princess. Just adapt the idea as you choose. A Google search should bring up a number of costume websites where you can find a costume to suit your purposes.

The store announces over the PA system that the bandit is in the kitchen department for the next 30 minutes offering a private home staging consultation at 10-20% off for the first 5 or 10 people who make a reservation or appointment.

You could test out different offers to find what works best. Or they could offer 20% off all kitchen remodels and a free home staging consultation besides. People often need to upgrade their kitchen before putting it on the market. If you did this at times when the store is busiest, do you think you'd probably discover some people in the store who are in need of selling their homes who would appreciate a staging consultation or who would gladly pay you to manage the entire project for them?

If there are no takers you can return later in the day and do it again, this time extending the time you'll be there to take reservations or altering the offer as you see fit.

Even if there are no signups to the offer right then, you have a chance to explain home staging to all who gather, hand out your business card or brochure and ask for referrals. You promise the store that any and all parts, cabinets, hardware, wood, or any other products needed in the course of doing a staging service would be purchased from the store and not any of their competitors.

Before you would make such a deal with the store, however, you need to tie up the rights to this idea so that no other stager in your area could come in with a similar idea and take business away from you. Be sure to tie up the rights BEFORE you test it out. Assuming it is a fabulous idea, you don't want to have to fight for your rights AFTER the store knows how well it works. You also want the store to post in conspicuous places ahead of the arrival a sign, both inside and outside, announcing the arrival of the bandit.

You could even pay a pro rata fee for a tag added to the store's regular advertising that tells people to be sure to be in the store on a specific day and at a specific time to meet and greet the bandit and get their marked down special coupons. You could even pass out coupons and allow people to take advantage of your staging services over the next 30 days or 60 days or 90 days or to even pass the coupon on to someone else if they like. Can you see how this could work for you?

If you put out any money for advertising, costume, signs and so forth, your agreement with the store is that any new revenue that comes from the bandit should go to you first until your costs are recuperated. This is referred to as **first monies**. In any deal of this nature, everyone gets their first monies out before profits are divided up. So if the store offers a discount for the bandit to give out, the store gets to recoup their hard costs before you would share in any revenue generated by the sales of the stores related products in that department.

Ideally your bandit could conceivably generate a higher volume of shoppers on the day the bandit is there which would entitle you to get a percentage of the increased profits made throughout the store that day, not just in the department where the bandit hangs out. Returning bandits could go to different departments: gardening, lighting, plumbing, indoor plants, paneling, carpeting and so forth. Once you have a proven method worked out, you can repeat this whole procedure in other stores all around the area. This one single idea could keep you busy all month or more if done correctly.

Before you try this out with a major retailer, it is wise to test it first at a smaller store with an honorable owner or manager who will share the numbers with you. Once you know the concept will generate a certain % of increased visitors, or increased sales or both, this will give you some reasonable figures to pass on to other stores where you anticipate even greater success. You could also demand that, assuming the idea is hot, that you receive a larger percentage or commission on future visits by the bandit.

But don't rely on this idea alone. Some times the best ideas come from industries and sectors of the economy that are completely unrelated to ours. What ideas can you come up with that you know have proven to be successful in other fields that you can bring over into the staging industry? If you come up with any, I'd appreciate hearing from you with the idea. Together we help each other for the benefit of everyone. You'll find my contact information at the end of this book. You can also go the opposite direction and turn your character into the Home Staging Bonus Bandit. By adding other values other than discounts, you can still accomplish the same goals. Choose other items in the store that have great profit margins. In your case you're discounting or giving bonuses on your time and talent, which means no money out of pocket for you. These products or services don't even have to be something the store owner sells currently. You can literally get products and services from other companies to use as a give away or bonus to setting an appointment with you.

You'd be amazed at how many companies will give you, literally give you all kinds of coupons you can give away which cost you nothing at all. The point is that they add perceived value to what you really want to transact.

Lastly, be sure to stress to the store owner that everyone who comes to sign up for an appointment will surely buy more products from the store in the process of you serving their staging needs. If it is a home improvement store, the conclusions are logical. All products needed to repair or spruce up the home will be purchased at their store, so the on-going profit potential is very strong. (Possibly use store coupons to guarantee they will come to the store.)

Make sure the store owner realizes that the true value of all these customers is in the repeat business that staging will generate for them now and down the road as well.

Heck, if you love playing the bandit or you have someone who is good at it, you could even syndicate the idea and provide bandit services for other types of businesses around town that are completely unrelated to staging. That's if you enjoy it. You could even sell the rights to use the idea to companies outside your area. You could visit a mall and get the mall association to bring you in on a specific day to visit every store in the mall. I'm just throwing out other ideas that have a low cost involved but could return huge profits, whether you tie the idea to your business or keep it separate.

Protecting Your Rights

Know that there is a very real hazard in many of the business deals I may recommend to you beyond whether they will be profitable or not. Realize that while you are validating your idea with another party, they may be stealing the idea right out from under you. This is why it is so important to protect your ideas on a written agreement **before** you start to share how powerful they are. A simple letter of agreement, written by your attorney, should cover you even if the other parties use it one time only. You stipulate that they may never use the idea again without paying you a fee equivalent to 50% of what they paid you on the first usage of your idea – or they can buy the idea outright from you for a lump sum.

In business there are, unfortunately, fewer honest people, truly honest, so you want to deal with the most reputable people you can find. The dishonest ones may misrepresent the numbers to you, or under report the actual sales generated or drag their feet when it comes to paying you. The more these issues are addressed up front in your agreement, the less likely you'll be to have problems.

Chapter Five
Handy Forms to Get You Ready

Broadbrush Assessment of Your Business

I love forms. They really help me organize my thoughts. They really help me dissect myself, my education, my experience, my background, my skills, my talents, my goals and so much more.

Forms help motivate me to put my information down on paper where I can analyze it, where I can add to it, where I can see the whole picture and not just the parts.

Forms are very practical. They are very useful.

Forms help you organize. They help you focus. They help you highlight what needs to be highlighted. They are precise. They force you to hone down to just the bare essentials because they often don't give you much space to write. This is good because you really have to boil all your thoughts, facts and figures down to their bare bones, basic reality.

From your forms you will be able to capture the essence of who you are, where you've been, where you're going and why. You'll be able to see things about yourself you didn't realize before. You'll be able to remind yourself of important aspects you had forgotten about.

They'll help you tie all the loose ends together and formulate your strategies and tactics in concise plans of action.

So don't neglect using the forms I have provided you here. Feel free to make photo copies. Use them. Work with them. Let them steer you. In the end, I guarantee you that you'll find them worthwhile. In the end I guarantee you'll come away with a new and deeper understanding of your self, your business, your goals and your future.

Broadbrush Assessment of My Business

Who are the people / businesses I want to reach?

_____
_____
_____
_____
_____
_____
_____

What other products, services and options do people typically purchase prior to buying or using my type of product / service?

_____
_____
_____
_____
_____
_____
_____

Who provides those products / services?

_____
_____
_____
_____

What products / services, etc., do people typically need and/or acquire along with or in order to optimally use my product or service?

_____
_____
_____
_____
_____
_____

Who provides those products / services?

_____
_____
_____
_____
_____
_____

What assets do I need that I do not have?

_____
_____
_____
_____
_____
_____
_____

What periodicals / advisory materials are used by the market I want to reach?

_____
_____
_____
_____

Who provides those products / services?

_____
_____
_____
_____
_____

What problem or opportunity does my product / service solve for my prospects/clients?

_____
_____
_____
_____
_____
_____
_____

What other type of business, organization, profession, etc., has more to gain than even I do by seeing me either acquire a client or sell a specific product, service, or combination, and why?

_____
_____

_____
_____
_____
_____
_____
_____

What other market or industry could use/benefit from my product, selling system or methodologies?

_____
_____
_____
_____
_____
_____

What is the Marginal Net Worth of my client/prospect worth to someone else?

_____
_____
_____
_____

What are my highest margin products or services?

_____
_____
_____
_____
_____

What are my highest repeat purchase products or services?

_____
_____
_____
_____
_____

What logical products can I create, acquire, adapt or adopt?

_____
_____
_____
_____

_____
_____
_____
_____
_____

What markets can my products or services also apply to or translate to?

_____
_____
_____
_____
_____

What related fields can I penetrate?

_____
_____
_____
_____
_____

What parallel universes are most similar to mine?

_____
_____
_____
_____
_____

What other business markets, products or services have I been thinking over?

_____
_____
_____
_____
_____

What else can I think of to maximize my leverage and monetize my worth?

_____
_____
_____
_____

Optimal Model Questionnaire

What are you really trying to do with your passive income activities?

_____
_____
_____
_____
_____
_____

What kind of specific deals are you most focused on trying to go for?

_____
_____
_____
_____
_____
_____

Why are you trying to do that?

_____
_____
_____
_____
_____

How much time do you **realistically** have available to do this RIGHT NOW?

_____
_____

What are your **relevant** strengths (pertaining to questions above)?

_____
_____
_____
_____
_____

What are your **relevant** weaknesses (pertaining to questions above)?

_____
_____
_____
_____

What industries or activities or areas do you want to concentrate on first? And why?

_____

_____

_____

_____

_____

_____

What part will YOU play in this transaction process? Who else and what other skill sets do you need to rely on to achieve your goal?

_____

_____

_____

_____

_____

_____

What size transactions do you want to target first? And why?

_____

_____

_____

_____

_____

_____

How are you going to know that these are reasonable and realistic goals for the deals?

_____

_____

_____

_____

_____

_____

Who is going to present the proposition / offer for you?

_____

_____

_____

_____

_____

_____

How are you / they going to present it? What form / method?

_____
_____
_____
_____
_____
_____

What follow up process or sequence will you / they use?

_____
_____
_____
_____
_____
_____

What are the key objections you have to be able to overcome or preempt?

_____
_____
_____
_____
_____
_____

Start reverse engineering the dynamics to see what metrics you need. What has to happen to make the vision real?

_____
_____
_____
_____
_____
_____

What is your time line and what actions need to take place?

_____
_____
_____
_____
_____
_____
_____
_____
_____

My Bartering Opportunities - Personal

WHAT DO I NEED?   WHO HAS IT?

My Bartering Opportunities - Business

WHAT DO I NEED?   WHO HAS IT?

My Bartering Opportunities - Personal

WHAT DO I HAVE?	WHO NEEDS IT?

My Bartering Opportunities - Business

WHAT DO I HAVE?   WHO NEEDS IT?

My Bartering Opportunities - Personal

WHAT DO I HAVE ACCESS TO? | WHO NEEDS IT?

My Bartering Opportunities - Business

WHAT DO I HAVE ACCESS TO? | WHO NEEDS IT?

My True Asset List

TANGIBLE ASSETS	INTANGIBLE ASSETS

My Skills List

PERFECTED SKILLS	MODERATE SKILLS

My Knowledge List

EXPERTISE/SPECIALIZATION	FAMILIARITY WITH

My Relationship List - 1

PEOPLE IN MY COMPANY	PEOPLE I'VE WORKED WITH IN PAST

My Relationship List - 2

MY FAMILY	MY FRIENDS

My Relationship List - 3

MY MENTORS | BUSINESS PEOPLE I KNOW

My Relationship List - 4

SCHOOL / COLLEGE FRIENDS	NEIGHBORS / PAST NEIGHBORS

My Relationship List - 5

PAST BUSINESS RELATIONSHIPS	PRESENT BUSINESS RELATIONSHIPS

My Relationship List - 6

PEOPLE I CURRENTLY REACH	COMPANIES TARGETING MY LIST

My Relationship List - 7

DEMOGRAPHICS I CURRENT REACH	OTHERS REACHING MY DEMOGRAPHIC

My Relationship List - 8

MY PSYCHOLOGICAL REACH	PSYCHOLOGICAL REACH OF OTHERS

My Relationship List - 9

MY CURRENT PRODUCTS	NEW RELATED PRODUCTS

My Relationship List - 10

MY CURRENT SERVICES	NEW RELATED SERVICES

My Relationship List - 11

RELATED COMPANIES	ABOUT TO GO OUT OF BUSINESS

My Relationship List - 12

MY COMPETITORS	ABOUT TO GO OUT OF BUSINESS

Yellow Pages Research - 1

BUSINESSES OF FAMILIARITY	BUSINESSES BY LOCALITY

Yellow Pages Research - 2

BUSINESSES BY PERSONALITY	BUSINESSES BY AFFLUENCE

Yellow Pages Research - 3

BUSINESSES BY DEMOGRAPHICS	OTHER BUSINESSES

Barter Scrip

I, _____ , on this day, _____

do hereby agree to perform the following service or trade the following product(s):

TYPE OF SERVICE   TYPE OF PRODUCT

_____

VALUE OF SERVICE $ _____   VALUE OF PRODUCT $ _____

TIME PERIOD IN WHICH SERVICE IS TO BE PERFORMED OR PRODUCT TRADED

_____

OTHER AGREEMENTS   □ TRANSFERRABLE   □ NON-TRANSFERABLE

_____
_____
_____

IN EXCHANGE FOR

_____
_____
_____
_____

TRADING PARTY #1   **TRADING PARTY #2**

_____   _____
Name   Name

_____   _____
Address   Address

_____   _____
City/State/Zip Code   City/State/Zip Code

_____   _____
Phone   Phone

_____   _____
Email Address   Email Address

_____   _____
Signature   Signature

Staging Scrip

I, _____ , on this day, _____

do hereby agree to perform the following home staging service:

TYPE OF SERVICE   □ NUMBER OF DAYS _____

VALUE OF SERVICE $ _____

TIME PERIOD IN WHICH SERVICE IS TO BE PERFORMED

OTHER AGREEMENTS   □ TRANSFERRABLE   □ NON-TRANSFERABLE

□ FURNITURE   □ ACCESSORIES   □ CLEANING   □ REPAIRING   □ DECLUTTERING
□ FURNITURE REARRANGEMENT   □ LANDSCAPING   □ CONSULTING   □ RENTAL PROPS
□ OTHER _____   □ OTHER _____

IN EXCHANGE FOR

_____

_____

_____

_____

TRADING PARTY #1   **TRADING PARTY #2**

_____   _____
Name   Name

_____   _____
Address   Address

_____   _____
City/State/Zip Code   City/State/Zip Code

_____   _____
Phone   Phone

_____   _____
Email Address   Email Address

_____   _____
Signature   Signature

Redesign Scrip

I, _____, on this day, _____

do hereby agree to perform the following redesign service:

TYPE OF SERVICE   □ Half Day Service   □ FULL DAY SERVICE

VALUE OF SERVICE $ _____

TIME PERIOD IN WHICH SERVICE IS TO BE PERFORMED

OTHER AGREEMENTS   □ TRANSFERRABLE   □ NON-TRANSFERABLE

_____
_____
_____
_____

IN EXCHANGE FOR

_____
_____
_____

TRADING PARTY #1   **TRADING PARTY #2**

_____   _____
Name   Name

_____   _____
Address   Address

_____   _____
City/State/Zip Code   City/State/Zip Code

_____   _____
Phone   Phone

_____   _____
Email Address   Email Address

_____   _____
Signature   Signature

139

Due Bill

A due bill is used whenever a trade is to be transacted in the future. It can be a simple statement of intent or a more formalized agreement. The best ones, I think, are the old fashioned kind that are simple to draw up and simply stated. Naturally the larger the trade, the less simple agreements tend to be.

The Due Bill should naturally have the date the agreement is signed, but should also have the expiration date as well. It should fully describe the products or services to be transacted. It should also be transferable and state the conditions under which it is transferable (if any).

It can be as simple as this:

I, _____ , located at
_____ promise
to trade

_____
_____
_____

to _____ , located at
_____

in exchange for

_____
_____
_____

This trade is transferable to anyone under the following conditions:

_____
_____
_____

Today's Date   Expiration Date

_____   _____

_____   _____

Signature of Party 1   Signature of Party 2

Consignment Agreement

This consignment agreement is between _____, represented by
_____ hereinafter referred to as Consignor and
_____ represented by
_____, hereinafter referred to as Consignee.

Consignor will provide the following merchandise on a consignment only basis to Consignee. Consignee will display the consigned merchandise in their business establishment in a predetermined and jointly approved location.

_____
_____
_____
_____
_____
_____
_____

TERMS OF AGREEMENT

Consignee agrees to be completely responsible for the goods once they are placed in the Consignee's designated location. Once a week Consignor will visit the location and together determine how many products have been purchased, restock the shelves or bins and make sure the space is attractive and organized.

Together Consignor and Consignee will keep an accurate record of sales. Each party will receive _____% of the net profit for the week/month as determined below. Consignor shall also receive the pre-determined wholesale price of the product in addition to Consignor's net profit.

□ Weekly   □ Monthly   □ Other _____

Damaged, lost or stolen merchandise shall be paid for by Consignee at the wholesale value, whose responsibility it is to provide reasonable security within the establishment.

DATE _____

_____   _____
NAME OF CONSIGNOR   NAME OF CONSIGNEE

_____   _____
ADDRESS   ADDRESS

_____   _____
CITY, STATE, ZIP CODE   CITY, STATE, ZIP CODE

_____   _____
SIGNATURE OF CONSIGNOR   SIGNATURE OF CONSIGNEE

Return on Investment (ROI)

As of this writing you should find the following percentages pretty accurate, according to www.homesalemaximizer.com and their HomeGain Maximizer. In a nationwide study conducted by HomeGain, real estate agents identified 10 top home improvements that can add thousands of dollars to the sale of a home for minimal cost. Typical percentages range from a low of 94% to a high of 837% depending on the improvement and what part of the country the home is situated in. HomeGain has divided the US into four sections: Eastern, Western, Southern and Midwest.

Here is a list of the types of improvements they have tracked for more than a decade.

- Lighten and brighten
- Clean and de-clutter
- Landscape front/back yards
- Stage home for sale
- Repair electrical and plumbing
- Repair damaged flooring
- Update kitchen and bathrooms
- Replace or shampoo carpeting
- Paint exterior walls
- Paint interior walls

On the following pages you'll find worksheets I've prepared to help you assist your client in determining the most valuable ways to maximize their budget. This is assuming the seller still lives on the property and will leave some furnishings for you to stage with. Obviously if the house is empty, more thought and consideration should be placed on renting furniture while the home remains on the market.

Disclaimer: These figures were taken from HomeGain's current study and may have changed dramatically since then, either upwards or downwards. So do contact them at the website above to get your own Maximizer that is as current as they have available.

Imagine! If a high percentage of agents recommend a specific task, you should recommend it as well. If a low percentage of agents recommend a task, think how much better the property will stand out if you recommend it and the seller does it or hires you to do it for them!

Your task is to maximize your client's budget and get them the most value and the most perceived value you can while staying within their budget. Focus on what is right for them and the rest will take care of itself.

Eastern ROI Worksheet

Enter the typical cost for each task in your locality and multiply that by the percent increase in your area to receive an approximate price increase they might expect to receive. Lastly enter the percentage of agents in your part of the country who would typically recommend this task be accomplished before listing the property.

- ## Lighten and brighten

TYPICAL COST	PRICE INCREASE	ROI	% OF AGENTS RECOMMENDING
		310%	96%

- ## Clean and de-clutter

TYPICAL COST	PRICE INCREASE	ROI	% OF AGENTS RECOMMENDING
		543%	97%

- ## Landscape front/back yards

TYPICAL COST	PRICE INCREASE	ROI	% OF AGENTS RECOMMENDING
		415%	95%

- ## Stage home for sale

TYPICAL COST	PRICE INCREASE	ROI	% OF AGENTS RECOMMENDING
		378%	93%

- ## Repair electrical and plumbing

TYPICAL COST	PRICE INCREASE	ROI	% OF AGENTS RECOMMENDING
		133%	96%

• Repair damaged flooring

TYPICAL COST	PRICE INCREASE	ROI	% OF AGENTS RECOMMENDING
		176%	97%

• Update kitchen and bathrooms

TYPICAL COST	PRICE INCREASE	ROI	% OF AGENTS RECOMMENDING
		140%	87%

• Replace or shampoo carpeting

TYPICAL COST	PRICE INCREASE	ROI	% OF AGENTS RECOMMENDING
		186%	99%

• Paint exterior walls

TYPICAL COST	PRICE INCREASE	ROI	% OF AGENTS RECOMMENDING
		194%	83%

• Paint interior walls

TYPICAL COST	PRICE INCREASE	ROI	% OF AGENTS RECOMMENDING
		190%	98%

Western ROI Worksheet

Enter the typical cost for each task in your locality and multiply that by the percent increase in your area to receive an approximate price increase they might expect to receive. Lastly enter the percentage of agents in your part of the country who would typically recommend this task be accomplished before listing the property.

• Lighten and brighten

TYPICAL COST	PRICE INCREASE	ROI	% OF AGENTS RECOMMENDING
		486%	95%

• Clean and de-clutter

TYPICAL COST	PRICE INCREASE	ROI	% OF AGENTS RECOMMENDING
		837%	96%

• Landscape front/back yards

TYPICAL COST	PRICE INCREASE	ROI	% OF AGENTS RECOMMENDING
		263%	95%

• Stage home for sale

TYPICAL COST	PRICE INCREASE	ROI	% OF AGENTS RECOMMENDING
		244%	86%

• Repair electrical and plumbing

TYPICAL COST	PRICE INCREASE	ROI	% OF AGENTS RECOMMENDING
		183%	86%

• Repair damaged flooring

TYPICAL COST	PRICE INCREASE	ROI	% OF AGENTS RECOMMENDING
		134%	89%

• Update kitchen and bathrooms

TYPICAL COST	PRICE INCREASE	ROI	% OF AGENTS RECOMMENDING
		148%	81%

• Replace or shampoo carpeting

TYPICAL COST	PRICE INCREASE	ROI	% OF AGENTS RECOMMENDING
		128%	96%

• Paint exterior walls

TYPICAL COST	PRICE INCREASE	ROI	% OF AGENTS RECOMMENDING
		121%	94%

• Paint interior walls

TYPICAL COST	PRICE INCREASE	ROI	% OF AGENTS RECOMMENDING
		134%	93%

Southern ROI Worksheet

Enter the typical cost for each task in your locality and multiply that by the percent increase in your area to receive an approximate price increase they might expect to receive. Lastly enter the percentage of agents in your part of the country who would typically recommend this task be accomplished before listing the property.

- ## Lighten and brighten

TYPICAL COST	PRICE INCREASE	ROI	% OF AGENTS RECOMMENDING
		355%	98%

- ## Clean and de-clutter

TYPICAL COST	PRICE INCREASE	ROI	% OF AGENTS RECOMMENDING
		605%	97%

- ## Landscape front/back yards

TYPICAL COST	PRICE INCREASE	ROI	% OF AGENTS RECOMMENDING
		298%	97%

- ## Stage home for sale

TYPICAL COST	PRICE INCREASE	ROI	% OF AGENTS RECOMMENDING
		456%	86%

- ## Repair electrical and plumbing

TYPICAL COST	PRICE INCREASE	ROI	% OF AGENTS RECOMMENDING
		201%	94%

- ## Repair damaged flooring

TYPICAL COST	PRICE INCREASE	ROI	% OF AGENTS RECOMMENDING
		136%	94%

- ## Update kitchen and bathrooms

TYPICAL COST	PRICE INCREASE	ROI	% OF AGENTS RECOMMENDING
		115%	88%

- ## Replace or shampoo carpeting

TYPICAL COST	PRICE INCREASE	ROI	% OF AGENTS RECOMMENDING
		176%	97%

- ## Paint exterior walls

TYPICAL COST	PRICE INCREASE	ROI	% OF AGENTS RECOMMENDING
		195%	91%

- ## Paint interior walls

TYPICAL COST	PRICE INCREASE	ROI	% OF AGENTS RECOMMENDING
		136%	96%

Midwestern ROI Worksheet

Enter the typical cost for each task in your locality and multiply that by the percent increase in your area to receive an approximate price increase they might expect to receive. Lastly enter the percentage of agents in your part of the country who would typically recommend this task be accomplished before listing the property.

• Lighten and brighten

TYPICAL COST	PRICE INCREASE	ROI	% OF AGENTS RECOMMENDING
		315%	100%

• Clean and de-clutter

TYPICAL COST	PRICE INCREASE	ROI	% OF AGENTS RECOMMENDING
		439%	100%

• Landscape front/back yards

TYPICAL COST	PRICE INCREASE	ROI	% OF AGENTS RECOMMENDING
		332%	98%

• Stage home for sale

TYPICAL COST	PRICE INCREASE	ROI	% OF AGENTS RECOMMENDING
		351%	99%

• Repair electrical and plumbing

TYPICAL COST	PRICE INCREASE	ROI	% OF AGENTS RECOMMENDING
		154%	97%

• Repair damaged flooring

TYPICAL COST	PRICE INCREASE	ROI	% OF AGENTS RECOMMENDING
		138%	97%

• Update kitchen and bathrooms

TYPICAL COST	PRICE INCREASE	ROI	% OF AGENTS RECOMMENDING
		88%	90%

• Replace or shampoo carpeting

TYPICAL COST	PRICE INCREASE	ROI	% OF AGENTS RECOMMENDING
		138%	99%

• Paint exterior walls

TYPICAL COST	PRICE INCREASE	ROI	% OF AGENTS RECOMMENDING
		94%	92%

• Paint interior walls

TYPICAL COST	PRICE INCREASE	ROI	% OF AGENTS RECOMMENDING
		144%	99%

Sample Forms

The following forms are currently approved by the State of California as of this writing. By displaying them here, I make no claim whatsoever as to their usefulness at the time you are reading this. Nor are these forms suitable for residents outside the State of California. I provide them here merely as samples and every reader of this guide is cautioned to check with their state (even in California) for the up-to-the-minute forms that are acceptable in their state or county. With that disclaimer in mind, please see the type of information one might typically find on the forms shown.

Use the first form when the claimant is required to execute a waiver and release in exchange for or in order to induce the payment of a progress payment and the claimant has not been paid. This form is useful when the claimant has not been paid yet, but will be paid out of a progress payment that is not the final payment. This conditional waiver and release is only effective if the claimant is actually paid.

CONDITIONAL WAIVER AND RELEASE UPON PROGRESS PAYMENT

Civil Code Section 3262(d)(1)

Upon receipt by the undersigned of a check from _____

MAKER OF CHECK

in the sum of $ _____ payable to _____

AMOUNT OF CHECK   PAYEE OR PAYEES OF CHECK

and when the check has been properly endorsed and has been paid by the bank upon which it

is drawn, this document shall become effective to release any mechanic's lien, stop notice, or

bond right the undersigned has on the job of _____

OWNER

located at _____ to the following extent.

JOB DESCRIPTION

This release covers a progress payment for labor, services, equipment, or material furnished to

_____ through _____

YOUR CUSTOMER   DATE

only and does not cover any retentions retained before or after the release date; extras furnished before the release date for which payment has not been received; extras or items furnished after the release date. Rights based upon work performed or items furnished under a written change order which has been fully executed by the parties prior to the release date are covered by this release unless specifically reserved by the claimant in this release. This release of any mechanic's lien, stop notice, or bond right shall not otherwise affect the contract rights, including rights between parties to the contract based upon a rescission, abandonment, or breach of the contract, or the right of the undersigned to recover compensation for furnished labor, services, equipment, or material covered by this release if that furnished labor, services, equipment, or material was not compensated by the progress payment.

Before any recipient of this document relies on it, said party should verify evidence of payment to the undersigned.

Dated:_____ _____

COMPANY NAME

By:_____

TITLE

NOTE: This form complies with the requirements of Civil Code Section 3262(d)(1). It is to be used by a party who applies for a progress payment when the progress check has not yet cleared the bank. This release only becomes effective when the check, properly endorsed, has cleared the bank.

7/04

UNCONDITIONAL WAIVER AND RELEASE UPON PROGRESS PAYMENT

Civil Code Section 3262(d)(2)

The undersigned has been paid and has received a progress payment in the sum of

$_____ for labor, services, equipment or material furnished to _____

YOUR CUSTOMER

on the job of _____ located at _____

OWNER   JOB DESCRIPTION

and does hereby release any mechanic's lien, stop notice or bond right that the undersigned has on the above referenced job to the following extent.

This release covers a progress payment for labor, services, equipment, or material furnished to

_____ through _____

YOUR CUSTOMER   DATE

only and does not cover any retentions retained before or after the release date; extras furnished before the release date for which payment has not been received; extras or items furnished after the release date. Rights based upon work performed or items furnished under a written change order which has been fully executed by the parties prior to the release date are covered by this release unless specifically reserved by the claimant in this release. This release of any mechanic's lien, stop notice, or bond right shall not otherwise affect the contract rights, including rights between parties to the contract based upon a rescission, abandonment, or breach of the contract, or the right of the undersigned to recover compensation for furnished labor, services, equipment, or material covered by this release if that furnished labor, services, equipment, or material was not compensated by the progress payment.

Dated:_____ _____

COMPANY NAME

By:_____

TITLE

NOTICE: THIS DOCUMENT WAIVES RIGHTS UNCONDITIONALLY AND STATES THAT YOU HAVE BEEN PAID FOR GIVING UP THOSE RIGHTS. THIS DOCUMENT IS ENFORCEABLE AGAINST YOU IF YOU SIGN IT, EVEN IF YOU HAVE NOT BEEN PAID. IF YOU HAVE NOT BEEN PAID, USE A CONDITIONAL RELEASE FORM.

NOTE: This form complies with the requirements of Civil Code Section 3262(d)(2). It is to be used to release claims to the extent that a progress payment has actually been received by the releasing party.

7/04

Use this form when the claimant is required to execute a waiver and release in exchange for or in order to induce the payment of a final payment and the claimant has not been paid. This release is only binding if there is evidence of payment to the claimant. Evidence of payment may be demonstrated by:

- the claimant's endorsement on a single check or a joint payee check which has been paid by the bank upon which it was drawn; or

- written acknowledgment of payment given by the claimant.

CONDITIONAL WAIVER AND RELEASE UPON FINAL PAYMENT

Civil Code Section 3262(d)(3)

Upon receipt by the undersigned of a check from _____

MAKER OF CHECK

in the sum of _____ payable to _____
$

AMOUNT OF CHECK   PAYEE OR PAYEES OF CHECK

and when the check has been properly endorsed and has been paid by the bank upon which it

is drawn, this document shall become effective to release any mechanic's lien, stop notice, or

bond right the undersigned has on the job of _____

OWNER

located at _____

JOB DESCRIPTION

This release covers the final payment to the undersigned for all labor, services, equipment, or

material furnished on the job, except for disputed claims for additional work in the amount of

$_____. Before any recipient of this document relies on it, the party should verify

evidence of payment to the undersigned.

Dated:_____ _____

COMPANY NAME

By:_____

TITLE

NOTE: This form of release complies with the requirements of Civil Code Section 3262(d)(3). It is not effective until the check that constitutes final payment has been properly endorsed and has cleared the bank. 7/04

Use this form when the claimant is required to execute a waiver and release in exchange for, or in order to induce payment of, a final payment and the claimant asserts in the waiver he or she has in fact been paid the final payment.

UNCONDITIONAL WAIVER AND RELEASE UPON FINAL PAYMENT

Civil Code Section 3262(d)(4)

The undersigned has been paid in full for all labor, services, equipment or material furnished

to _____ on the job of _____
         YOUR CUSTOMER   OWNER

located at _____ and does hereby waive and release any right to a
                    JOB DESCRIPTION

mechanic's lien, stop notice, or any right against a labor and material bond on the job, except

for disputed claims for extra work in the amount of $_____.

Dated:_____   _____
                                                                  COMPANY NAME

                                       By:_____
                                                                  TITLE

NOTICE: THIS DOCUMENT WAIVES RIGHTS UNCONDITIONALLY AND STATES THAT YOU HAVE BEEN PAID FOR GIVING UP THOSE RIGHTS. THIS DOCUMENT IS ENFORCEABLE AGAINST YOU IF YOU SIGN IT, EVEN IF YOU HAVE NOT BEEN PAID. IF YOU HAVE NOT BEEN PAID, USE A CONDITIONAL RELEASE FORM.

NOTE: This form complies with the requirements of Civil Code Section 3262(d)(4). It is to be used to release claims to the extent that a progress payment has actually been received by the releasing party.

7/04

Sample Confidentiality Agreement

THIS AGREEMENT is made and entered into as of this _____ day of _____ ("Effective Date"), by and between _____, a _____ Corporation with its principal place of business at

_____

_____

_____

_____, and _____ ("Vendor") a _____ corporation with its principal place of business at

_____

_____

_____.

In an effort to explore working together on real estate related technology products for _____would like to provide_Vendor with information and materials about its business and operations and may request similar information from Vendor Evaluation Materials, whether it be in a tangible form (e.g. and without limitation, written or printed documents, computer disks or tapes) or a non-tangible form (e.g. and without limitation, information communicated orally), includes but is not limited to any and all intellectual property or trade secrets, software, information concerning research, design details and specifications, financial information, customer lists, business forecasts, and marketing plans. In consideration of our agreement to furnish each other with such Evaluation Materials, each of us hereby agrees as follows:

Confidentiality. The Evaluation Materials will only be made available to those of the parties' directors, officers, employees, advisors, and agents. The Representatives receiving the Evaluation Materials may reproduce, summarize, and use such Evaluation Materials only for the purpose of evaluating the relationship. The Representatives agree to keep all Evaluation Materials confidential, not to disclose or release the Evaluation Materials other than to Representatives and not to use the Evaluation Materials in any manner materially detrimental to the other party. The Evaluation Materials disclosed hereunder are and shall remain the property of the disclosing party and no license or other rights in or to such information, including rights under any trade secrets, copyrights or patents, is granted to the receiving party.

Evaluation Materials. The term "Evaluation Materials" does not include information which (i) at the time of disclosure or thereafter is generally available to and known by the public (other than as a result of its disclosure by the receiving party or its Representatives), (ii) was available to the receiving party on a non-confidential basis from a source other than the disclosing party or its advisors, or (iii) has been independently acquired or developed by the receiving party without violating any of its obligations under this Agreement.

Required Disclosure.   In the event the receiving party or any of its Representatives are requested pursuant to, or required by, applicable law, regulation or legal process to disclose any of the Evaluation Materials, the receiving party will notify the disclosing party promptly so the disclosing party may seek a protective order or other appropriate remedy or, in the disclosing party's sole discretion, waive compliance with the terms of this Agreement. In the event no such protective order or other remedy is obtained, or the disclosing party waives compliance with the terms of this Agreement, the receiving party will furnish only that portion of the Evaluation Materials which it is advised by counsel is legally required and will exercise all reasonable efforts to obtain reliable assurance that confidential treatment will be accorded the Evaluation Materials.

Termination.   This Agreement shall commence as of the Effective Date. Either party may terminate this Agreement upon written notice to the other party. Upon termination, the receiving party will return to the disclosing party the original and all copies of the Evaluation Materials in the receiving party's possession or in the possession of its Representatives, or at the request of the disclosing party, the receiving party will destroy the original and all copies of any analyses, compilations, studies or other documents prepared by it or for its internal use which reflect the Evaluation Materials. Each party shall certify in writing that it has returned all original and duplicated Evaluation Materials or, if requested, destroyed the original and all copies of any analyses, compilations, studies or other documents prepared by it or for its internal use which reflect the Evaluation Materials. The receiving party will hold the Evaluation Materials in confidence for a period of three (3) years from the Effective Date.

No Publicity. Each of us agrees, unless otherwise required by law, or mutually agreed upon by both parties, not to disclose to any other person the fact that the Evaluation Materials has been made available to us, or any of the specific terms or conditions with regard to the Possible Transaction, including the existence and status thereof.

Representation or Warranty. Each of us understands and acknowledges that although the Evaluation Materials contains information which the disclosing party believes to be accurate and relevant for the purpose of the receiving party's evaluation of the Possible Transaction, the disclosing party and its Representatives do not make any representation or warranty, expressed or implied, as to the accuracy or completeness of the Evaluation Materials. Each of us agrees that neither the disclosing party nor its Representatives shall have any responsibility to the receiving party or any of its Representatives relating to or arising from the use of the Evaluation Materials, except as may be specifically provided in any agreement we may subsequently execute.

No Obligation to Consummate Possible Transaction. Each of us agrees that unless and until a definitive agreement between us with respect to the Possible Transaction has been executed and delivered, neither party will be under any legal obligation of any kind with respect to such a transaction by virtue of this Agreement or any written or oral expression with respect to such a transaction by any of its Representatives, except, in the case of this Agreement, for the matters specifically agreed to herein.

Specific Performance. Any breach of our mutual understanding with respect to publicity or any breach of our confidentiality undertaking by anyone making any disclosure or misappropriation of Evaluation Materials could cause irreparable harm to the non-breaching party, the amount of which would be extremely difficult to estimate. Accordingly, it is understood and agreed that monetary damages would not be a sufficient remedy for any material breach of this Agreement and that specific performance and injunctive relief shall be appropriate remedies for any such breach or any threat of breach. The remedies discussed above shall not be deemed to be the exclusive remedies for any such breach of this Agreement but shall be in addition to all other remedies available at law or in equity.

Limitations. Each of us agrees and understands that each reserves the right in its sole discretion to undertake a similar initial review or analysis with other third parties. Further, the terms of confidentiality under this Agreement shall not be construed to limit either party's right to independently develop or acquire products without use of the other party's Evaluation Materials. Each party that receives Evaluation Materials agrees that it will not use such information in any way that is detrimental to the disclosing party. The parties may decide at any time without notice either to restrict the transfer of information to the other party, to reject any and all proposals, or to modify or terminate evaluation of the Possible Transaction.

Entire Contract. This Agreement is intended to constitute and constitutes the entire agreement of the parties. Its terms are intended by the parties as a final, complete and exclusive expression of the parties with respect to its subject matter and may not be contradicted by evidence of any prior or contemporaneous oral agreement.

Amendments and Waivers. This Agreement may be amended or modified, and any of the terms or covenants hereof may be waived, only by a written instrument duly executed by each of the parties hereto, or in the case of a waiver, executed by the party waiving compliance.

Attorneys' Fees and Applicable Law. If either party employs attorneys (or utilizes in-house attorneys) to enforce any rights arising out of or relating to this Agreement, the prevailing party shall be entitled to recover reasonable attorneys' fees. This Agreement shall be governed by, and construed in accordance with, the laws of the State of California, excluding conflict of laws principles. The parties to this Agreement acknowledge and understand this Agreement is entered into in the State of California, the County of Los Angeles, to be performed herein, and any judicial action brought in connection with this Agreement, whether in law or equity, shall be filed exclusively in a court of competent jurisdiction located within the County of Los Angeles, the State of California and decided in accordance with the substantive and procedural law of the State of California.

Severability. If any provisions of this Agreement, or the application thereof to any person, place or circumstance, shall be held by a court of competent jurisdiction to be invalid, unenforceable or void, the remainder of this Agreement and such provisions as applied to other persons, places or circumstances shall remain in full force and effect.

Successors and Assigns. Subject to the limitations set forth in this Agreement, this Agreement will inure to the benefit of and be binding upon the parties, their successors and assigns.

IN WITNESS WHEREOF, and intending to be legally bound hereby, the parties have caused this Agreement to be duly executed by their authorized representatives as of the Effective Date.

_____   _____
Signature   Signature

By:_____   By:_____

Name: _____   Name: _____

Title:_____   Title: _____

Sample Copy for a Staging and Redesign Website

Welcome to luxury without leaving home!

In today's world we spend less time enjoying our homes and families and focus on work, shopping and the news of yesterday's events. Often times we watch the rich and famous highlight their homes on TV. How we wish we could one day be able to live the life of luxury.

The beautiful home, well designed curb appeal, the huge fish pond with the different tropical fishes swimming around - imagine changing your space to reflect what is shown on TV for the rich and famous - or even the ordinary, average people. Would that be a dream come true?

Please let me introduce myself to you.

My name is _____. I am the owner of _____. I've had a life long passion for decorating since I was a child. I have always rearranged my grandparent's furniture in their homes to play doll house with my friends.

Growing up I continued with my passions decorating for friends, acquaintances and family, giving decorating tips and ideas whenever possible. But I bring more to the home staging and redesign projects that I accept.

I enrolled with the **Academy of Staging and Redesign** (Decorate-Redecorate.Com) and completed the necessary course to become a Certified Staging Specialist & Certified Redesign Specialist. It required me to pass a lengthy exam and submit a portfolio of my work for professional review and passage before receiving my designation.

I am also currently a member of _____ and continue to expand my education and training every year so that my services are on the cutting edge of staging and redesign and what's happening in my industry.

I can assist you with placing your furniture correctly, picking the right color for your fabric, walls, or accessories or just give you the advice you need to make your space warm and inviting.

My Mission:
1. I aim to please. My goal is always to do what is in my client's best interest – whatever it takes to ensure their complete and utter satisfaction and the results we have jointly set out to achieve.

2. To eliminate all the hassles from my client's lives as pertains to their home and their full enjoyment of it.

About Me.

My goal is to perform the best feasible design available. I am not an interior designer but a home stager (redesigner). I use your furniture to re-decorate your home to look amazingly beautiful and fully functional. If you wish I can assist with purchasing new furniture to furnish your space so that it will be comfortable and inviting to friends and family. I will also create special designs for pets. With the extensive training from the Academy of Staging and Redesign and previous design experience you can be assured of getting excellent services that will exceed all your expectations, hopes and dreams for your home.

Services

Real Estate and Home Staging Consultation and Services
Real Estate Redesign Services
Redesign Consultation and Services
Move in Design and Arrangement Services
Color Consultations
Personal Shopping Services
Holiday and Specialty Services

Real Estate Consultant:

For the homeowners that would prefer to handle their home improvements but need professional feedback to market their homes
_____ will be very happy to provide the home owners with all the necessary information to upgrade and receive the best offers in the shortest time frames.

Real Estate Redesign:

First impressions are very important to a buyer!
_____can assist you with creating an unforgettable look to your home by removing unwanted furniture and de-cluttering to make a space appealing to buyers. Consultation fees will be discussed during initial home evaluation.

Redesign Consultation:

_____ consultant will visit your home and perform an in-depth inspection, get familiar with your space and develop an action plan to rearrange your space into a divine look.

Redesign Service:

_____ consultant will remove unwanted furniture at owner's request and replace with new furniture to meet homeowner's budget. Prior to signing of agreement for services, fees will be thoroughly discussed.

Design Consultation:

_____ consultant will assist clients with proper paint color choices, wall paper, window treatments, upholstery fabrics, flooring, furniture, bedding, lighting fixtures and wall decorations and more. Fees vary.

Move –In Design and Arrangement:

_____ will assist with coordinating your new space from moving into your new home, apartment, condo, retirement, vacant home. Consultant can give you the deserving look and feel you want and deserve.

Color Consultant:

Paint can be one of the most difficult liquids to work with especially when affected so easily by lighting changes and adjacent colors in the room. _____ consultant will work with you to select the correct color to blend with your selections of decorations and accessories. Fees vary.

Personal Shopping:

Shopping can be very time consuming especially when you do not know where to locate what you are looking for. _____ consultant is available to purchase all your home furnishing and accessory needs at your request. Fees vary.

Holiday and Specialty Service:

Looking forward to the holiday spirit but do not have the time to shop for those holidays decorations? _____ consultant will decorate your inside and outside to reflect your taste and style, all suitable for the neighborhood as well. Fees vary.

Staging Benefits

Staging is an investment for home owners and real estate agents to justify higher asking prices. It is for home owners that want to de-clutter, depersonalize and rearrange furniture and accessories to change the look and feel of the home so it will appeal to the broadest pool of potential buyers.

Redesign Benefits

Giving a room a complete make over does not always require expensive new furniture and accessories. Most rooms already have the resources needed for great design. Transform your space using your own furniture and accessories combined with new paints, lighting and art. Creates a beautiful functional space that reflects your personal style and not that of the redesigner.

Contact Us

Name [ ]

City [ ]

Phone [ ]

Email [ ]

Your are a [Select... ▼]

Services (Select all applicable) ☐ Home Staging

☐ Vacant Home Staging

☐ Model Home Staging

☐ Holiday/Event Staging

☐ Move-in Decorating

☐ Organizational Solutions

☐ Color Consultation

Timing [Immediate ▼]

Best Time to Reach You [Select... ▼]

Comments [ ]

[Submit]

Chapter Six

How to Hire Vendors During Tough Times or Any Time for That Matter

How to Hire a Handyman

Hiring a handyman is not easy and many people have had bad experiences with handymen. Complaints usually include such things as they don't show up, they don't return calls, they say they can do the work but end up disappointing their clients.

However, there are scores of people who have had wonderful experiences hiring those "small job" workmen. Sometimes it's a communication failure. In such cases the fault lies with both sides.

But before we go further, let's first discuss what a handyman does.

What is a Handyman?

The handyman profession is not easy to define. Not all handymen are the same and they definitely have different skill sets and they have different preferences of the type of work they will accept. So one needs to quiz each person to find out what skills they say they have and try to acquire evidence that they do, indeed, have the skills they claim to have before hiring them.

Those skills could include chores such as: electrical repairs, plumbing repairs, tile work, lock smith, painting walls, painting the house and so forth. Technically speaking most people would say that a handyman is someone who knows how to perform odd jobs, small jobs mostly, and a wide variety of jobs. They tend to specialize in nothing and are adept at doing a myriad of things. In reality they may also be looking for the large projects but are willing to take on small projects when jobs are scarce. They have bills to pay just like everyone else.

What Can a Handyman Do?

One thing that is certain - a "handyman" should not be defined by his skills alone.

All handymen are not skilled in all things They come from all walks of life and all sorts of interesting backgrounds. Some handymen come from a trade background with primary skills in carpentry or the construction trades. A few are electricians and plumbers, though not as many since the money is usually better in those licensed and often unionized professions. Some are tile installers or roofers or appliance repair people who, as mentioned earlier, fill in the lean times with handy-work from their current customers or referrals.

But all handymen are not from the trades and not all handymen are skilled in crafts. Some are just honest hard-working people willing to do a day's work for a day's pay. Some will ply their trade raking leaves, cleaning out your basement - anything to make some money. Others don't have many skills now but want to learn and seek to become "freelance apprentices". They wish to become educated on-the-job and often charge relatively low rates for the opportunity to gain experience while working on your home.

And let's not forget the illegal workers who are willing to do anything whether they are skilled or not and want to be paid in cash so there is no record of them earning any money so they can escape the IRS as well as immigration services. Often this is where a lot of problems arise due to language difficulties where communication is almost non existent. Buyer beware.

What Are a Handyman's Skills?

Here is the first truism about the handyman profession - a handyman's skills are defined by what that specific handyman can do. You definitely cannot lump all handymen into the same basket. Since there is no standard handyman profile, each handyman brings to your home different abilities and capabilities. The handyman-roofer may do a great job cleaning gutters or replacing a door lock, but keep him away from the garbage disposal and the toilets. That great handyman/carpenter will professionally renovate your small basement but don't let him near the broken bicycle or the garage door opener.

Here is what a handyman is:

1. A handyman is defined as a person that can do the job or jobs you need done around your home – to one degree or another.
2. A handyman is not capable of doing everything - so pressuring a handyman to do work he is not comfortable with may lead to disappointment.
3. Handymen come in all flavors, sexes, ages and sizes. It's not just a male profession any more as there are handywomen rising up to challenge this once male dominated profession. Though many think of handymen as retirees or part-timers supplementing their incomes, the fact is that thousands of people of all ages are professional "handy people" who make their living through this work.
4. So there are professional and part-time handymen. A pro will most likely have wider experience and hence be a little more costly to hire. A part-time handyman will have a more narrow range of skills but may be more reasonably priced.

Rules for Hiring a Handyman (or Handywoman)

If you skipped to this section, please go back and read the above paragraphs so the rest of this section will make sense to you. You don't want to make a mistake about hiring a handyman for your own home and you certainly don't want to recommend someone to your clients who does inferior work or who is unreliable or who has trouble communicating in the language of your client.

Rule #1 - Have a clear idea of what you want... and make a list!

With such a broad reaching profession, it is incumbent on you to ask the right questions of your handyman if you expect to hire or recommend intelligently. Before even considering calling, get together a list of the things you want done or that you recommend your client have done. In this "laundry list" or "stager list" you want to list the tasks in the order of priority, if you can.

Though there are many handymen with a tremendous range of skills you can't assume anything. It is important to go over the list with the handyman later in the screening process. Your goal is to decide if this person will do enough of your work to make hiring him worthwhile. You will need to know if you'll need to bring more than one handyman in to work on the project. Ideally you want to hire someone who can do it all, but this may be impractical or even impossible.

Rule #2 - Develop a list of handymen prospects

The easy way to start your search is to pick up the local newspaper or "Pennysaver" and look through the home repair classifieds. Angieslist.com is also a large online source of handymen and other service providers across the country. You can also do an online search in your area for people to contact by entering the word "handymen" along with your city and state in the search bar. However, the downside is that many successful handymen do not advertise. After a few years in business, many multi-skilled, full-time handymen find themselves overwhelmed with new business and stop actively promoting themselves and have failed to even list their business on such online sites. They don't have to advertise because of their personal networking and referrals from multiple sources that keep them busy year round.

So how do you find these handyman gems? Try soliciting the help of lumberyards, condo associations and hardware stores. Talk to your neighbors, family, friends and co-workers. Talk to other vendors and suppliers of home improvement products. Many of these businesses and organizations keep lists of tradesmen that they refer. Many are very careful who they list and will remove a tradesman if they receive any negative reports.

There are even online websites that list handymen and give the clients a way to give feedback on the service they received. Obviously it should go without saying that if you find one getting a lot of negative feedback that it would be best to avoid them, particularly if you need them for a client's home.

Here's another point to remember. Just because one company or handyman did a good job on one aspect of a project, that does not mean they will do excellent work on every aspect of a job. It doesn't even mean they would do excellent work on any future project. So you have to ferret out the good from the poor ones on the type of tasks you need done from one project to another and never totally rely on past performance as a gauge of future performance.

Needless to say, one of the best ways to start the search is to receive a trusted referral from a friend, relative or business associate. This type of referral makes the screening process a little easier since you have some information about the handyman before you talk to him on the phone or have him standing at your front door. But remember what I just wrote above - that just because a handyman did a great job for one client yesterday, today is a whole new day and a new client and no two projects are ever alike.

Consider joining HandymanClub.Com to learn more or make contacts.

Rule #3 - You must ask these questions!

1. **Request at least a few references... and then be sure to check out the references.**

   This isn't as important with a direct, trusted referral but it is vital if you pick your handyman out through advertisements in newspapers, mail or over the Internet. Remember... you are inviting this person into your home for your own projects and into the home of your clients on their projects. Caution is the rule of the day.

2. **Ask direct questions about the handyman's experience, training and ability.**

   How many years has he or she been in business? Since most handymen are male, I will use that pronoun from here on out. What are his favorite jobs? Don't be shy to ask questions because your clients will expect you to choose wisely. You have to know the full scope of the handyman's business. Ask if he has ever had a job go wrong, what happened and how he resolved it. If he says he has never had any problems ever, this is probably not the truth. Everyone has a job that does not go as planned every once in a while. You want to find someone who is honest as well as capable.

3. **Find out about business licenses, resale licenses and insurance.**

   Every state has different rules concerning licensing and registration for home repair contractors and all businesses are expected to abide by the laws of the state, county and city. Because "handy-work" often crosses many crafts and the jobs can be quite small, laws that apply to builders and contractors may not apply to handymen in your locale. For example, some states require licensing for **all** contractors; some rules are based on the average size of the job, others are based on the contractor's annual income and some states require nothing at all! In some large metropolitan areas, the rules can vary literally from block to block as strange as that seems. Some states defer to local governments. To determine the licensing requirements for your area, call your local building inspector or town hall or visit your civic center.

4. **How does the handyman price his work? Does he give FREE estimates? Charge by the hour or half hour?**

   This is another issue that may be at least partially regulated by the state or local government. Some states require written quotations for jobs over a certain dollar amount. This is to protect consumers from unscrupulous contractors who give a "ballpark" price and jack up the price after the client is committed and "in too deep". For small jobs, many handymen charge by the hour - usually with a minimum charge. Make note of his hourly rates. When comparing handymen, realize that the hourly rate can be a reflection of his experience, how popular he is and his overhead costs. In my experience, though, there is often little connection between the hourly rate and the skill of the handyman. Frequently, pricing is based as much on what the market will bear and the competition's rates than some unexplainable formula.

Never give "carte blanche' to anyone. If you have an upper limit regarding spending for the project, let the handyman know up front. He should be able to help you understand what is required, what could go right and, more importantly, what could go wrong to drive the price beyond your budget. With this honest exchange of information, there will hopefully be no surprises for either you or your client. Get all this in writing.

5. **Contractor liability insurance is NOT optional on some projects.**

Though the job size may be small, a little mistake can lead to a big disaster. Your handyman should have some sort of liability insurance coverage. It is not unreasonable to ask for proof of insurance. The really good ones may carry their documentation with them or have copies to hand you without even being asked. This is the exception however. Some may stare at you blankly when you ask for copies of this documentation. That's a clue that the person is not on top of his business or may be working on the "fringe". If the project is very simple and straight forward like having someone rake the leaves or haul away trash, you need not be too strict or demanding. Use common sense and you should be fine.

6. **Get credit references, social security or Federal ID numbers. and bank references.**

Unless you want your handyman to take on a big job such as building a deck or a small renovation, credit and bank references are not really necessary. Many reputable handymen run a "cash" business and don't have established credit or loan histories relating to their business. However if they are lawful US citizens, they will have a social security number if they are a sole proprietor. If they are incorporated, they will be able to give you their Federal Employee number. This is important because during a time when we want to promote work for US citizens, this is another way to weed out the illegal workers from the legal ones.

Do not settle on a workman because he appears to be the cheapest. There is a saying that Judge Millian (People's Court) often says in Spanish: "The cheap comes out expensive." People who conduct their business bypassing the legal steps (business cards, references, business license, bonds and insurance) are often hiding from deportation, the IRS or other official governmental oversight entities. Hiring them may not only be against the law, but could open you or your client up to problems you don't need or want. By the way, this advice is good for hiring anyone regardless of the type of business they operate.

7. **Check for consumer complaints against the handyman.**

It is important that you call the local Better Business Bureau, the local Chamber of Commerce and the state licensing agencies. But if you don't find any complaints, that's a good sign but you need to know that people who suffer inferior workmanship are often too embarrassed to report it.

Good handymen have worked for hundreds of homeowners repairing the mistakes or the omissions of other contractors, yet when they ask the client if a complaint was ever filed, the answer is usually "no". Some are just weary after months of broken promises and disappointments. They just want the problem to be over. In the end, most just accept their dismal fate, hire other people to correct the mistakes, and silently let the bad behavior continue within the community.

On the other hand, many complaints filed by consumers are not really serious but instead stem from either misunderstandings or "power plays". A customer may complain because the cost of a job increased after the customer made a midstream change in the plans. Another customer may decide to change the location of a window after it was already installed, expecting the contractor to absorb the additional labor costs. Some consumer complaints are out and out frauds – they are instead attempts to delay payment or get cost concessions from the handyman or contractor. Complaints should be weighed after hearing both sides if that is possible.

Before You Call the Handyman:

- Walk through your home and list the small repairs needed. E.g.: dripping faucet, loose cabinet doors, faulty light switch, etc.
- Get organized before you make the call. Keep a list of all repairs needed in your job records so you can give the repair person a good idea of the job size before they come to your home or to your client's home.

- Make a list of other items of concern or ones you think might get worse.
- Decide if you or your client will be able to afford all the repairs at once or if they need to be done in phases. If in phases, prioritize them.

When Your Handyman Arrives:

- Walk through your client's home and describe each of the repairs to the handyman.
- Decide on an hourly or per job rate. Realize that most firms front load the first hour and that some repair people are famous for showing up to look over a job, then claiming they have to go get a part, only to go to the next job, then come back and expect to "get paid for their travel time". Since you know this is a common practice, let the handyman know from the outset that if you are to work together or recommend him for a project that this kind of behavior will not be tolerated. Let him know that you expect him to arrive fully capable of doing the project right on the first visit, such as repairing the door on a dryer. A good and honest repairman will ask enough questions over the phone to know what to bring to do the job. There should never be any reason to have to go get something "back at the office" or from some other source. Do not tolerate anyone on your "team" who pads their time sheet in order to boost the price for you or for your client.
- Ask for references and examples of other jobs if you still aren't sure about his work – and do so even if you are sure. Check and double-check and thoroughly do your research, especially in a down economy when the temptation for those who are unethical is to lie, cheat and steal from clients.

How to Hire a Contractor

Get Recommendations From Others

Start with your friends and family and neighbors and ask for their recommendations. Chances are you'll pick up a name or two of a reputable company. You can also go to: (**nari.org/homeowners/findapro**) which is the National Association of the Remodeling Industry for a list of members in your area. Other ideas are to talk with building inspectors. They will know which contractors routinely meet code requirements and

which ones don't. You can also visit your local lumberyards and home improvement stores. They know which ones buy quality materials, make purchases on a regular basis and pay their bills on time.

Conduct Your Own Phone Interviews

Once you've created a list, make a quick call to each of your prospects and ask them the following questions:

- Do they take on projects of your size?
- Are they willing to provide financial references from suppliers or banks?
- Are they licensed, insured and bonded?
  Can they give you a list of previous clients?
  How long have they worked with their subcontractors?
- Are their workers employees or do they use day laborers from the community?
  How many other projects would they have going at the same time?

The answers to these questions will reveal the company's availability, reliability, their legal status, how much attention they'll be able to give your project and how smoothly the work will go. It isn't an exact science that will totally protect you or your client from having difficulty, but it will go a long way to helping you minimize the hazards of hiring the wrong company.

Meet Them Personally

Never hire a company without first meeting the principles face to face. Based on your phone interviews, pick three or four representatives to meet with you so you can discuss your needs further and acquire estimates. But before you do that, check with your state's consumer protection agency and the local Better Business Bureau to see if your prospects have a history of disputes either with their clients or with other subcontractors. Whenever possible, meet with the owner or president, not just with a salesman. Even though you like the salesman, he will not be the person you will ultimately deal with and you want to be comfortable with whoever the company will assign to manage your projects. If you find there is a long negative history about any company, cross it off your list. Make sure there is always going to be someone on site who speaks excellent English (or your client's native language).

The person you meet with should be able to answer all of your questions satisfactorily and in a professional manner. It is crucial that you be able to communicate completely and easily with this person as communication is essential for any project to progress satisfactorily. Do not make decisions based on someone's personality.

Investigate the Facts Before You Hire Anyone

Now that you have narrowed down your list you can put all this research to good use. Phone the former clients of the contractor to find out how their project went, how it was concluded, and ask to see the finished product. But don't rely on results alone. Even more importantly, visit a current job site and see for yourself how the contractor works and how he interfaces with those at the job site. Is the job site neat and safe? Are workers courteous and careful with the homeowner's property? Sometimes it's better to visit when you know the contractor will not be present and no one knows who you are.

Make Plans, Get Bids and Evaluate

After you have your short list of contractors whose track records appear clean and whose work ethic looks responsible, it's time to proceed. Stop looking back at past work and start looking forward to your client's project. One of the advantages you will have is that you will be seen as good source to future work, so in most cases a contractor will really want to impress you. However, please note that it is human nature, after a few projects have been completed, for a contractor or subcontractor to get complacent and lower their attention to detail. So it's important to make sure they know from the outset that you will keep close tabs on all work for every project – and then be sure to do just that.

A conscientious contractor will want not only to complete a set of blueprints but also to get a sense of what your clients want out of a project and what they plan to spend. To compare bids, ask everyone to break down the cost of materials, labor, profit margins and other expenses in their bids. You want, as much as possible, to be able to compare "apples to apples" and "oranges to oranges". Generally materials may account for 40 percent of the total cost (depending on the price of commodities at the time) - the rest will cover their overhead and their typical profit margin (likely to be 15% to 20%).

Don't Let Prices be Your Main Consideration

Discard the lowest bid if it is substantially lower than the others. This contractor is probably cutting corners or overly desperate for work – a bad sign in a good economy. However, in a bad economy all rules must be more carefully evaluated. You still want to hire a company that will still be in business to complete the project, so even though you may have sympathy for a company that is struggling, you owe it to your client to choose a company that is capable of weathering downturns in the economy. After making sure of their technical competence, you want to feel comfortable with your choice – you want to have peace of mind. Never forget this - the single most important factor in choosing a contractor is how well you and he communicate. All things being equal, it's better to spend more and get someone you can easily communicate with.

Make Them Put Everything in Writing

By law the person who draws up the contract is responsible and has the liability should any part of it be ambiguous. If you draw it up, you are ultimately responsible if there is a communication problem. So draw up a contract that details every step of the project: 1) prices and payment schedule; 2) proof of liability insurance, contractor's license, business license and worker's compensation payments; 3) a start date and projected completion date; 4) what happens if the completion date is passed with work still to be done; 5) specific materials and products to be used; 6) a requirement that the contractor obtain lien releases from all subcontractors and suppliers (which protect you if he doesn't pay his bills); 7) how surprises or unintended consequences will be managed; 8) what happens if changes need to be made during the project or after its conclusion and so forth.

Insisting on a clear and specific contract isn't about mistrust – it's about insuring a successful end result for all parties concerned. Remember that as soon as a change is made or a problem uncovered, the price just automatically increased and the project just got longer. So tell your client that the four most expensive words in the English language are: "While you're at it . . ."

Set Up a Payment Schedule

In California it is illegal for a contractor to require pre-payment of more than 10% of the job. Your state may have different requirements or none at all. Whether your client is able to prepay a project or not, never prepay any more than the law requires. More people have run into problems before, during and after a project because they foolishly prepaid the contractor just because they were asked to do so. Instead, insist on a payment schedule.

Payment schedules will speak to a contractor's financial status and work ethic. If they want half the bid up front, they may have financial problems or be worried that you won't pay the rest after you've seen their work. Here is a good rule of thumb to follow. For large projects, consider a schedule of 10 percent at contract signing, three payments of 25 percent evenly spaced over the duration of the project and a check for the final 15 percent when you feel every item on the project's list has been completed. This keeps the contractor happy and it gives you or your client plenty of leverage if things start to deteriorate.

Following are some examples of a mechanics lien and release. These are important documents to get signed where appropriate because you do not want your client (nor you) to be responsible for paying for materials or labor that your contractor was supposed to pay for. Some unfortunate homeowners have been stuck twice for the cost of materials and labor. They paid their contractor who was supposed to pay his suppliers and subcontractors from the contract but failed to do so. Those suppliers and subcontractors then came after the homeowner to pay them. Since the homeowner benefited directly from the materials and labor, they were on the hook to pay again since they did not get the proper releases. Do not neglect this area.

DISCLAIMER: Check with your own state, county or city to make sure you have the proper form. The examples at the end of Chapter Five are purely examples and I cannot guarantee their suitability for any project. These are <u>only</u> examples.

Mechanics Lien and Release (See Chapter 5 for Forms)

<u>General Principles:</u> No lien release is binding unless the claimant executes (signs) and delivers a waiver and release. If signed by the claimant or his or her authorized agent, the signed form is effective to release:

- the owner
- the construction lender; and
- the surety (in the case of a payment bond).

<u>Be careful:</u> paying your contractor (and/or getting a release from your contractor) does not guarantee that other claimants, like subcontractors and suppliers, are paid. A claimant is a person who, if not paid, can file a lien on the home that received the benefit of materials or labor. To be effective, the proper waiver and release forms must be used. The four forms are:

<u>Conditional Waiver and Release Upon Progress Payment</u>

Use this form when the claimant is required to execute a waiver and release in exchange for or in order to induce the payment of a progress payment and the claimant has not been paid. This form is useful when the claimant has not been paid yet, but will be paid out of a progress payment that is not the final payment. This conditional waiver and release is only effective if the claimant is <u>actually</u> paid. This release does not cover all items.

Unconditional Waiver and Release Upon Progress Payment

Use this form when the claimant is required to execute a waiver and release in exchange for or in order to induce payment of a progress payment and the claimant asserts in the waiver that he or she has in fact been paid the progress payment. This release does not cover all items.

Conditional Waiver and Release Upon Final Payment

Use this form when the claimant is required to execute a waiver and release in exchange for or in order to induce the payment of a final payment and the claimant has not been paid. This release is only binding if there is evidence of payment to the claimant. Evidence of payment may be demonstrated by:

- the claimant's endorsement on a single check or a joint payee check which has been paid by the bank upon which it was drawn
- written acknowledgment of payment given by the claimant

Unconditional Waiver and Release Upon Final Payment

Use this form when the claimant is required to execute a waiver and release in exchange for, or in order to induce payment of, a final payment <u>and</u> the claimant asserts in the waiver he or she has in fact been paid the final payment.

Caution: in the case of a conditional release, the release is only binding if there is evidence of payment to the claimant. Evidence of payment may be demonstrated by

- the claimant's endorsement on a single check or a joint payee check which has been paid by the bank upon which it was drawn
- written acknowledgment of payment given by the claimant

Sample forms are provided in Chapter Five. These types of forms should be considered any time a contractor or sub-contractor does work that involves bringing in materials (which are purchased elsewhere) or uses sub-contractors (that are to be paid by the company you hire). Don't get caught having to pay for products or services twice because you failed (or your client failed) to get these important documents signed by the companies hired.

How to Hire a Landscaper

How do you hire a landscaper? Or a tree trimming service? One thing is for sure. Don't hire a tree trimmer who stops by your home with alcohol on the breath. There's no telling what your tree will look like afterwards and it could be permanently ruined. So do what we've stated previously and first acquire referrals, particularly from your neighbors or your client's neighbors. Even if everyone you talk to makes good recommendations, your tastes and requirements are individual. The style of the home can also play a factor in the style of landscape that is most desirable. Then there is that matter of communication. Many contractors in this particular industry hail from foreign countries and their ability to communicate may be limited. You do want to hire someone you can communicate your desires and needs to and who can communicate with you just as easily. Choose well.

Knowing what you want done is key to a successful outcome. So the first task is to define the need before talking to anyone. Below is a list of tasks that typically are associated with landscaping and landscapers:

- Design
- Grading
- Drainage
- Erosion Control
- Soil amendment
- Irrigation
- Planting trees and shrubs
- Lawn sodding or seeding
- Hardscape – walks, walls, patios, decks, driveways
- Seasonal gardens
- Night lighting
- Water gardens
- Mulch
- Maintenance
- Pest control
- Tree evaluation, pruning, or management
- Tree and root removal
- Lawn care – mowing, edging, blowing, fertilizing

Ride around your neighborhood or your client's neighborhood and look for landscaping details that appeal to you. Ask neighbors for the contact information of their landscaper. Good professional landscapers depend a lot on referrals from satisfied clients and will welcome servicing you as well, assuming they have time available.

But you need to know that there are different types of landscapers and many items require them to have licenses and may also involve permits. Since the requirements differ from state to state, I cannot provide specifics here but merely a general overview. Each reader of should find out the requirements within their own state boundaries before proceeding to hire anyone.

Legal requirements:

Landscape Architect – Anyone using the title Landscape Architect or engaged in the practice of landscape architecture must be a Registered Landscape Architect. This law is a "practice act" regulating the practice of landscape architecture as well as the use of the title. Landscape architects tend to work on a large palette, designing malls and subdivisions for traffic flow, water movement, building placement, and things like that. Many landscape architects never study plant materials – but there are always exceptions! A few will work on smaller scale projects so you would have to ask to get an answer.

Landscape Contractor – Anyone using the title Landscape Contractor must be registered by the Landscape Contractors Registration Board. This law is a "title act" regulating the use of the title only. Anyone who thinks they can do the work can set themselves up in business as a "landscaper," "landscape installer," or "landscape designer." But to use the title "Landscape Contractor" requires passing exams covering soils, grading, plants and a number of other topics.

General Contractor - For projects including grading, building, public utilities, improvements, or structure with a cost exceeding a specific amount requires a license as a General Contractor.

Pesticide Applicator – A pesticide applicator's license is required for any applicator that applies a pesticide to control weeds, insects, plant diseases, or other pest control products for compensation. They may use the same product that you could buy to do it yourself. But if they do it as part of the job, then they must be licensed. That means they pass an exam, pay their fees, and attend recertification training. Even if they "only use over the counter type products" they must be licensed.

Credentials:

Some landscape professionals also pursue other credentials or certifications. These titles usually indicate some demonstrated knowledge of subject matter sufficient to pass an exam. Some of these include but may not be limited to: certified plant professionals, certified landscape technicians, certified turf grass professionals, certified arborists. Each of these certifications is offered by a professional association and has its own requirements.

Many professionals will also be members of one or more organizations. While membership usually only requires paying a fee, it often indicates that the business or individual is a participating member of the profession. It's one of the things professionals do for professional benefits as well as for continuing education opportunities.

Education:

Some high school graduates have received training in horticultural practices sufficient to enter the landscape business. Others pursue college degrees. "Green industry" professionals may have one or more degrees from colleges or universities in crop science, horticulture, arboriculture, environmental science, or related fields. Knowledge of plant science may provide a solid understanding for applying principles of plant management.

Experience:

Many "green industry" practitioners start out with "a pick-up and a mower." In some cases, that is all they have to recommend themselves. However, from just such a start, some of these same individuals have been in business for 10 or 20 years or more and may have learned a lot the hard way.

It is up to you to determine where a potential service provider started and how far he or she has come. No single qualification is the one that makes the difference; none carries a guarantee of satisfaction. Taken together, they all contribute to a professional approach.

The Job Agreement:

A good service provider should ask what you want.

The more you know what you want, the easier it will be to get it. But since you aren't likely to know all of the questions to ask, it is helpful for the landscaper to ask you questions, such as: What do you bring to the table? Do you need a design? Do you have a good idea of what you want? Do you need installation?

How about maintenance? All of the above? Are there specific plants you want or don't want? What is the size of the family and what are their outdoor activities?

A knowledgeable green industry practitioner may be able to help you verbalize your own ideas and visions. He or she may bring into the conversation words and terms that are new to you. Collect pictures of things that you like from magazines, take pictures of homes in the neighborhoods nearby that have features you like. Do some online searches for specific styles of landscaping or home styles. Nothing helps convey your wishes better than a good picture.

Make a list of what you want and share it with your landscaper. Be sure to keep a copy for your records. Don't neglect to ask or state the "obvious". You never know when your conceptualization will be different from what the landscaper conceptualizes. Terminology such as "natural" has tripped up more than one project. There are no silly questions when it comes to truly communicating what you want and what you expect to get.

How will the work be done?

Scheduling is one specific area that needs to be discussed thoroughly and understood. Weather is an obvious factor that may affect not only working conditions but also the end result. Rain and temperature cannot be controlled nor easily predicted and can throw off the schedule. Soil that is worked when it is very wet or very dry may suffer damage that can take years to overcome. There are optimal times for certain planting activities. You may have to find a balance between your immediate needs and your service provider's professional judgment about the optimal time of year for long-term success. Impatience can work against the final results.

Certain activities are better done in an order for efficiency of cost and labor. If you really need the lawn before an open house next week, it can probably be done for a price. If you want the lawn for the long term, however, it's more practical to install the irrigation system beneath it first, rather than tearing up the lawn to do it later. Some landscapers will subcontract certain portions of a job to sub-contractors. These service providers often find that someone who specializes in irrigation or large tree maintenance may provide you a better result at the same or lower cost or may speed up the schedule to meet your needs. You should want to know if multiple business operators will be visiting the property.

What will the investment cost?

Ask yourself this question: If my client can't afford to do it right, how can they afford to do it over? If your client is pressing to cut corners, pose the question to them. Much of the work of landscaping can be done by unskilled labor. However understanding where a plant is likely to survive best or not survive at all, understanding how to interpret a soil analysis, or understanding how plants can die slowly over time when poorly installed requires professional involvement. Your service provider should have liability and workmen's compensation insurance, including other fixed costs such as equipment and vehicle expense. Running a business includes many costs that are not obvious to people who have never had a business of their own.

Seek to find the right price that makes each party feel satisfied. It's one thing to negotiate a fair price and it is another thing to grind a price that really only benefits one side. The risk of doing so may compromise the standard of excellence, attention to detail and scheduling. It's only human nature to be tempted to cut corners when the reward one is to receive is less than it should be. So make every attempt to be fair to all parties in your negotiations.

Having said that, no matter what the cost, you can get it done cheaper.

If the cheapest possible price is your client's objective, you can save yourself and the professional a lot of time and frustration by stating that up front. Many reputable landscapers pride themselves on trying to do the cheapest job.

Whatever the cost, if you or your client is paying the bill, you have a right to know what you are paying for specifically. Different companies may itemize that differently. Ask the service provider to completely separate materials and labor. Some will want to offer a price based on a plant in the ground or finished mulching. If you don't like the way the company does business and you cannot get them to quote you in the manner you wish, it's a good idea to abort this agreement before it's signed. When comparing quotes between one company and another, you want to be fair to all parties and compare quotes given in similar formats. If you and the service provider have discussed what will be done, how and when it will be done, what it will cost, and how it will be billed and paid, then there should be few unpleasant surprises down the road – weather permitting.

Some Final Things to Think About

No garden or landscape is ever complete. The completion of an installation is actually the beginning of a landscape garden. Plants are living, growing things. The best of designs and installations can quickly "go to seed" without good maintenance. Someone needs to be out there every week monitoring and working on the landscape – especially if the house doesn't sell right away. If you don't plan for that, then you must certainly be disappointed. A landscape is not a product – it is a living, breathing entity that requires nurturing and care on a regular basis, especially before an open house.

Many customers want plants guaranteed to live. Life doesn't give us any guarantees. A plant is a living thing that has certain requirements for its life processes to continue. Many of these cannot be provided in advance. Those who provide the long-term maintenance will provide the best plant guarantee. They pay attention to plant water needs and adjust the irrigation. They monitor for early signs of disease or insect problems. They prune to shape and direct plant growth. They continue to guarantee that the plant gets what it needs. Your client can pay for that service, or they can do it themselves. I don't think it is reasonable to expect every plant that goes in the ground to live for even an entire year. Businesses that offer maintenance contracts may guarantee that plants will survive for a given period. Other businesses will offer only an occasional inspection and perhaps certain suggestions for action. But the long-term success of the landscape depends on the maintenance or lack thereof.

If a plant is dormant when it is planted in fall or winter, then it is reasonable to expect it to break dormancy the following spring. Beyond that, you can expect all plants will die eventually, so the more they are properly maintained the longer they will live. A landscape continues to change. As plants grow they create more shade, which changes the environment. Other plants may benefit or suffer as a result. The plant's water needs will change. While an attractive landscape may be a work of art, it is never a finished painting that we expect to be the same forever. It's a living organism. In its infancy it may require more work than later, but each landscape is as unique as a human being and deserves to be treated uniquely.

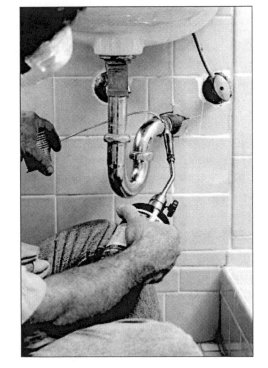

How to Hire a Plumber

Much like purchasing a car, finding a qualified plumber requires research and comparison shopping just as you have already learned from the prior discussions. Your first task, of course, is to clearly identify exactly what type of work needs to be done. Just as any other profession, the plumbing profession is not a one size fits all. There are plumbers who specialize in certain types of work and others who specialize in other types.

Just as before, the first step in finding a good plumber is to ask family and friends for recommendations of professionals they've hired in the past. Other good sources of referrals include contractors, real estate agents and your local plumbing supply store. Your city may even be able to provide a list of recommended plumbers who are familiar with the codes in your area. Since codes change depending on location, this is an important consideration.

There are two different types of plumbers -- those who handle repairs and those who specialize in new construction and remodeling. Repair plumbers should be called in for such items as clogged sinks, leaky faucets or emergency situations. The second type of plumber works on larger projects like replacing failed plumbing throughout the home or plumbing a new addition.
When asking for referrals, be sure to check the type of job the plumber was called in to accomplish. Determine if the plumber specializes in residential or commercial work as this can make a huge difference.

What to Look For in a Qualified Plumber

There are a number of qualifications which can set a professional plumber apart from other plumbers.

• State License or Certification -- Many states require a license or state certification for plumbers working in that state. Call to verify that the license is current and check if there are any active complaints against the license.

• Insurance -- Be sure that the prospective plumber you are considering is fully insured, having both workers' compensation and liability insurance. Your selected plumber should be able to provide you with a copy of his or her insurance policy and make sure the policy is still in effect.

• Better Business Bureau -- Contact your local Better Business Bureau to ascertain if any complaints have been filed against your potential candidate. If they have a website, go to the website. Read about the company and any guarantees they offer. Print off a copy. BBB memberships and the ability to check their rating may be available from links on their website. (Actually this is a good idea to do with all other service providers you ever consider as well.)

Questions to Ask

When you have narrowed the list, ask two or three plumbers to your home to survey the job and provide a written estimate that includes a materials list. The contract should spell out the scope of the project, any items that are excluded and the payment terms and schedule.

When obtaining a quote, one of the most important questions to ask your plumber is the type of materials to be used. Remember, a plumbing part defect has the potential to cause water damage to your home or your client's home or create an indoor swimming pool in what once was a basement.

Verify that the materials they propose using are in keeping with the codes. Ask for advice from your local home improvement plumbing department as if you would be doing the work yourself. Then compare what you are told with what each plumber states they will use. Don't be afraid to ask a lot of questions.

Quality Materials

Don't let your plumber install products made with inexpensive and inferior materials. Ask for quality materials, often with recognizable brand names that offer manufacturers' warranties for your client. You may pay more for these parts initially, but you will be glad you did if there ever is a problem or parts need replacing.

Reliability and Proven Performance

Become familiar with alternative materials on the market. Don't let a plumber repair a problem using the same materials that have already failed once. Ask your potential plumbing candidates whether they use any of the proven superior alternatives to copper. One such product is FlowGuard Gold CPVC pipe and fittings.

According to FlowGuard, "They are made of durable chlorinated polyvinyl chloride; these pipe and fittings offer a number of benefits over copper pipe. Mainly they will never scale, corrode or pit which will help eliminate the risk of future failures and costly re-piping. As compared to metallic systems, FlowGuard Gold CPVC systems also virtually eliminate condensation, significantly reducing the risk of costly drip damage to walls, structure and contents. From a health standpoint, the CPVC alternative offers the added benefit of maintaining water quality since there is no metal to leach into the tap water." In addition to inquiring about quality materials, other questions to ask a potential plumber include:

Length in Business and Their References

Ask each plumber how long he or she has been in business and if he/she has not been personally referred, ask to speak to several people who can vouch for the quality of their work and whether they completed the work on time and within budget.

Permits

Be sure to ask the plumbing professional to obtain all necessary permits.

Service Guarantees

Does the plumber guarantee the work? This is an important point if there are any problems that need fixing after initial installation. Service guarantees aren't just important for plumbing but for any work you have done.

Safety Commitment

Accidents can happen with almost any home improvement project. So ask your prospective service provider what steps he or she will take to prevent injuries and property damage. A common problem when installing copper pipe is a solder torch that gets too close to dry wall or wood joists in tight spaces. Non-metallic alternatives, like CPVC pipe, are solvent cemented (not soldered). The risk of fire is eliminated.

Clean Up

Ask the plumber how he or she intends to leave the work area once the job is completed. You don't want your client to clean up after a plumber for hours after they've left the home. As a home stager, you may be working on a home that is vacant and the owner out of the area in which case the clean up work would be up to you and probably would not be something you could add to your contract after the fact. Also ask about disruption during the project. For instance, if the plumber uses CPVC pipe, you won't have to worry about metal/copper filings to pick up or oil that may spill on your client's carpet or flooring.

Pricing

Compare prices, but remember the cheapest quote isn't necessarily the best plumber for the job. An experienced, qualified plumber may charge more for the work, but could save your client money in the end by doing the job right and using the best materials.

How to Hire a Cleaning Service

Having a house cleaner or maid service is a dream come true for a stager. Unfortunately for some, hiring a good house cleaning service

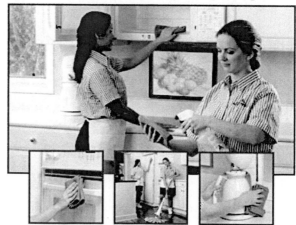

becomes a nightmare. Use this valuable information to avoid the pitfalls and find a quality house cleaning service that will keep your client's home sparkling clean and give you peace of mind. When staging a property, you will often be under time pressure and to clean the home yourself could be a lengthy process. It is often more advantageous to hire a professional cleaning service to take care of such chores. That leaves you free to manage the whole project more efficiently and get on to the more creative parts of your service just that much sooner.

Before You Start, Consider These Issues

Determine the frequency of service desired.
- One time
- Move-In
- Move-Out
- On-Call Cleanings
- Regular Service (Weekly, Bi-Monthly, Monthly)

Know the Special Needs
- Do you have a time of day preference?
- The days you or your client have available for cleaning
- Do you want only certain portions of the home cleaned or the entire home cleaned?
- Does anyone have chemical sensitivities or allergies?
- Does the cleaning need to be performed within 72 hours or just before an open house?

Decide Which Type of House Cleaner to Hire
- <u>Hire a company that has house cleaning sub-contractors.</u> You are not an employer but your relationship with the house cleaning company is arms length.
- <u>Hire a professional house cleaning company with employees</u>. This option provides you with the most service and support.

Learn more about each of these options to see which fits your client's needs best. Use the checklist when you interview companies.

What to Know Before You Hire Companies with Sub-Contractors

- The person who comes to the home needs to have a business license. Find out if they have <u>liability insurance</u>. For ongoing service it is recommended that you require insurance be mailed or faxed to you or client. This proves coverage is current. Failure to have insurance means your client would have to file against their own insurance company or pay out of pocket if the cleaning company damages anything.

- Will written cleaning instructions be necessary for each cleaning?
- What happens if the person assigned to clean gets sick, goes on a vacation, has car trouble, quits or gets fired?
- What happens if you or your client is unhappy with the cleaning?
- What is their policy if you want a different person to clean?
- For your client's protection: Before first cleaning, go through the house with the cleaner to find out what they plan to use on various surfaces. Inexperienced cleaners could use the wrong products or use the right products improperly. This can cause permanent damage or stains to your client's property.
- Will the work be paid by the hour or job? A good cleaner will try to complete all work requested and adjust the quality accordingly. Avoid getting someone who spends too much time in a section of the home.
- Will you get an invoice or will it be sent to your client? It is never wise to pay by cash or without an official invoice. Many undocumented workers want to be paid in cash. This is illegal and poor business practice to do so. It also makes it more difficult to use the expense as a tax write-off.

What to Expect From a Professional Service with Employees

Hiring a professional service with employees is usually the easiest and most relaxing way to get your client's home cleaned.

- They hire, train, insure and exchange employees as needed
- Housecleaners are employees of the company. They take care of all payroll and taxes so you and your client don't have to fret.
- They provide instructions to their employees about how the home should be cleaned.
- Most provide the cleaning supplies and equipment. Your client won't need to stock inventory or provide equipment.
- They have enough personnel to provide regularly scheduled cleaning. You don't want someone to fail to show up just before an open house.

What to Ask when You Interview

Here are some helpful questions to ask when you interview companies or candidates:

- Will they provide service as often as you or your client wants?
- Can they provide services to meet your special needs?
- Are employees covered by Labor & Industries if they get hurt?
- Do they hire undocumented workers?

- Does the company perform background checks on each employee? Are they bonded and insured?
- What type of training do employees receive?
- What takes place when something is broken, damaged, lost or stolen?
- Would they agree to have their insurance company send you or your client a <u>certificate of insurance coverage</u>?
- Do you or your client need to leave detailed instructions prior to each cleaning?
- Who's cleaning supplies and vacuum will be used?
- What happens if the scheduled cleaning falls on a holiday or weekend?
- What is the procedure if you or your client is not happy?
- Do they send the same employee each time?
- What happens if the employee is sick, on vacation, quits or gets fired?
- What actions does company take to provide consistently good quality?
- Why should their company be selected over their competitors?
- How often are customer cleanings rescheduled due to lack of employees, broken equipment, car problems and so forth?
- What are the charges for their services? Are there any hidden fees?

How to Rent Furnishings for Vacant Homes

Many homes you will want to stage are already vacant. The owners have already moved out, sometimes even moving out of state. So you are left staring at a shell – a blank slate – and it is up to you to decide what should be brought into the home to stage it properly.

Many of these decisions will be governed by the budget you have for the project. Some homeowners will be reluctant to spend anything at all to their detriment. In these situations it is your job to thoroughly explain the benefits they will get by letting you bring in rented furniture that is suitable for the style, size and economic level of the property. At first it is like solving a puzzle. You've got to look for all the pieces you need for each room that will be staged.

You've got to know in advance how you will arrange the pieces that are rented. This means you've got to have a good idea of the appropriate sizes so that you don't bring in furnishings that are too big or under scale for the room and the area you have to work with.

If the home is in a middle class neighborhood, the furnishings should be in keeping with the socio-economics of the home's location. If, however, the home lies in a high end community, the furnishings you bring in should complement the affluence of the area and the style of the home. It is important that potential buyers are left with the impression that the furniture in the home was owned by the homeowner, so your choices should reflect the style and color palette of the home as much as possible.

The size and scale of the furniture should fit the size and scale of the individual rooms. While your intent is not to fill the house up with furniture, you also do not want your choices to look dwarfed by the space. If the rooms are large, look for overstuffed furniture. If the rooms are small, look for non-upholstered pieces with open arms and open legs.

Know What You Need for Each Room

Selecting the wrong furniture for a room can have disastrous end results. You do not want to make poor choices that have to be returned to the rental agency. So to properly decide what you need, do the following:

1) Take pictures of each room from all angles, just as you would do for your future portfolio. Be sure to include views of the room's focal points.
2) Measure each room's width and length. Measure the individual walls and windows, recessed areas, closets, sliding doors, doorways and so forth. Note where there are doors, windows, vents, wall plugs, switches.
3) Note where all invisible walls are located, where the flooring changes from carpet to hard surfaces, the color palette of each room and the purpose you want to assign each room. Some bedrooms might have other usages you want to suggest, like a home business, a play room, a crafts room, or other activity besides a bedroom.
4) Reconstruct the dimensions and all the notations you have made for each room on graph paper. Using paper templates or one of our furniture planning kits or software, make a scaled drawing of the furniture you think you will need for each room.
5) Note that you don't have to fill up each room. You'll want to concentrate on the most important rooms in the home (living room, family room, dining room, master bedroom), but you can certainly scale down to vignettes in the other rooms. Your goal is to "suggest" how the

individual rooms can be used by a new family and help buyers fall in love with the house.

6) Write on your drawing the potential size you feel will work best and the colors you will need. Take your plan with you to the furniture rental company if you do not have what you need from your own personal resources.

7) Trust the decisions you made while you were in the residence. Try to find what you need without sacrificing on size or color. Choosing a style that blends with the style of the home is great, but in my opinion it is less important than having the right size and color. The reason is that in the end, the room must look and "feel" good to the buyer. If the size is out of whack (way too big or way too small) it will not "feel" right. Never forget that people purchase homes largely out of how they are made to "feel" and often toss out their list of requirements because they fall in love with how the home "looks". As a stager it is your job to facilitate those feelings and help them develop within the buyer by how you stage each room. The goal is to get every buyer to want the home so desperately that they are willing to pay top dollar to get it.

Unfortunately, no one can tell you exactly what to get for any project. You have to rely on the design training you have received to determine what is appropriate for your project. Every project is totally unique and different and, of course, your budget will change as well. It's important to work within your budget. But if you have a tight budget with a fixed amount, spend your quality dollars on the most important rooms (the high focus rooms): the common rooms plus master bedroom. If there is money left over, use it for the other rooms but not until you are satisfied that you have designed the important rooms the way they should be done.

Selecting the Right Furniture Rental Company

Preferably you have already selected one or more companies in advance of getting your first project and have made yourself aware of what they have to offer, their terms, their contracts and their pricing. This advance knowledge will help allay apprehensions during your planning and design phase. It will also speed up the process of getting what you want when you want it. (Photo opposite is from Cort.Com)

Here are some details you should nail down:

1) Pricing for various types of furniture
2) Pricing for "package" or "bundled" programs
3) Minimum rental periods
4) Pick up and delivery choices
5) Insurance and liability requirements and provisions
6) Installers or lack thereof
7) Variety, styles and colors to choose from and routine availability
8) Distance from property
9) Access to accessories or lack thereof
10) Required deposits, if any
11) Exit strategies, refunds, resolution methods

Be sure to familiarize yourself with the company's entire inventory in advance so you'll have a good idea which company you will probably need to contract the project to the moment you enter the home. Some well known national or regional rental companies are:

1) Brook Furniture Rental   www.bfr.com
2) Cort Furniture Rental   www.cort.com
3) Fashion Furniture Rental (So Cal) www.fashionfurniture.com
4) Rent Furniture (eastern states) www.rentfurniture.com
5) Furniture Rental Source   www.furniturerentalsource.com
6) Welcome Home Furniture   www.welcomehomefurniture.com

These are by no means the only companies out there that can meet your needs. For other companies, enter the words "furniture rental companies" and your city and state in the search bar of your browser and it should produce the contact information for companies in your area.

Rental companies have their own contracts that guarantee to protect THEIR rights and not yours and not the rights of your clients. So be sure to read everything in the contract to make sure you know what is required of you and/or your clients. And remember, just because something appears in a contract does not mean it cannot be negotiated. Most people accept contracts at face value and never even try to negotiate on any of the points they don't like.

It would be a good idea to collect the contracts from several nearby rental companies. Make an appointment with a local attorney and have him/her preview each contract to see if there is anything contained within that would seriously jeopardize your business before you accept a contract developed by another company. They are protecting their rights, not yours.

Even if you cannot get a term or requirement removed from a contract, through the negotiating process you might be able to secure some stipulation that protects you or your clients and makes the contract acceptable to all parties. But if you don't try, you definitely won't get it.

Rental of Accessories

In most cases I recommend you plan on stocking your own accessories. They are not as expensive to inventory, they don't take a lot of space, and they will allow you to make additional income. But if you don't have accessories and don't wish to purchase any, the rental company should have some you can add to the contract.

Places to pick up accessories include: garage sales, thrift stores, estate sales, online discount stores, your local department stores, discards from family and friends, sales from stagers or retailers going out of business or moving. Try to build up an inventory of neutral products (white, black, beige, brown) which would be suitable in almost any décor.
Do not invest in super expensive pieces since accessories can easily be stolen, broken or lost.
Make sure you keep an accurate inventory, including date purchased, where bought, price, size, color, rental value and so forth. This way you'll always have an accurate record of what you have and be able to assign a rental price for each item in keeping with its function and value. Once placed in a client's home, take pictures of all items placed for your records and insurance purposes. Note in advance any defects on any of the products. If possible, do a walk through with the client (or at least the agent) and have them sign your inventory and condition record, just as a precaution.

Virtual Home Staging - A Possible Solution for Empty Rooms When Budget is a Problems

Having written extensively on how to rent furniture and accessories in this guide and others, I now want to mention another option which you might like or dislike depending on your point of view.

Believe it or not, you can arrange to have your client's home staged virtually. Yes, the furniture and accessories are not real, but by golly it's pretty hard to tell that it's not real. A company has emerged who has online software that will accept your photos of the empty rooms (which have to be taken from a specific vantage point). See example here. You upload the photos to their server and they will create a fully furnished "virtually staged" image in return which you, the real estate agent or the seller can use to market the home.

Naturally you want to inform everyone that the rooms are <u>virtually</u> staged because you don't want a buyer to feel fooled once they arrive to see the home is actually empty. Now here is a picture of a virtually staged room. Please do not write me and ask how you can acquire this software. The company provides the service for you for a fee and does not allow others to use their

software. I mention this option here merely as another way to solve a problem for staging empty rooms in cases where rental of furniture is impossible or there is no other way to service the client's needs.

There is a fee for a base number of rooms and one can pay a little extra to have more rooms done. As a stager, you would let your client know this service is available and that you can handle everything for them. You charge them a fee slightly higher than it costs you, take the photos, upload them, get the staged ones back and make them available to your client. It's a reasonable solution for sellers who don't have the budget to hire you for actual staging services or for those that just refuse to spend adequate money or who may have a time crunch. Bear in mind this service is not for homes that already have furniture in them – only for empty houses. Naturally the results for actual staging are better than for virtual staging, because in most cases, that client will walk through the

door to see the home itself. However, for more details on this type of service (which I do not provide), please visit the following page: http://www.decorate-redecorate.com/virtual-staging-solutions.html

Chapter Seven
Closing Thoughts in Tough Times

The "process" is what life and business or talent is all about. This is as good as it gets - and that's wonderful, because each and every day, each and every hour, each and every person you interact with, each and every activity, challenge, problem you face is a wonderful opportunity to discover, to experience, to grow, to master. And what you will find is every day will be a success. Every day will be exhilarating.

Every day you'll give and you'll get.

The force multiplier effect is constantly at work if you think about it. Look at this illustration. Every time you tell someone about your business and they tell someone and they tell someone, can you not see the multiplying effect that is put into play immediately? It can be astounding.

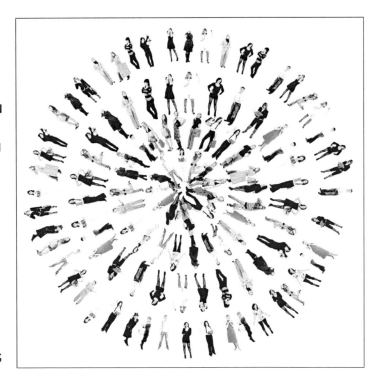

The essence of power and leverage with relationships in life is simply this:

Most people have it all backwards. They're struggling and striving to be interest<u>ing</u>, when all you have to do is turn it around. If you are interest<u>ed</u> in others, genuinely, you will endear yourself. You will stand out so favorably and incomparably, and you will learn so much that will broaden your understanding, and your mindset, and your knowledge – and your power.

I Can't Make You Successful

If you want to be a great home stager or dealmaker or broker or barter whiz, you've got to do the work. There's no other way around it. Of course you could always hire someone to do the work for you, but in tough times, that choice could very well be out of the question. If you have unsold time on your hands, do something about it. You'd be amazed at how much difference it can make.

During tough times, almost everyone struggles more and are ripe for someone to come along with an alternative way of doing business that is a viable (and maybe even more so) than cash transactions. Those people who are savvy enough and creative enough to see the deals and put them together will probably outdistance their competition and develop a strong, viable business in the process.

Anyone can be a deal maker, whether dealing for their own business or for other businesses. If you think you can't do it, then you're probably selling yourself short. This is serious work. If you're not prepared to apply serious effort to it, you should probably reconsider your whole path. The evidence of your commitment is in your actions, not your words.

Start with just making a paper deal – a deal on paper. If you can't even do that you'll never make an actual deal. I'm not into failure. I want you to be enormously successful but I can't make it happen for you. So my attempt here has been to give you as many fresh and innovative ideas, nuances, tools and suggestions to help you along the path to success in your staging business (or even apart from it).

Remember, I'm teaching you to be a deal maker, a barter whiz, a marketing superstar. I'm not teaching you to be a salesperson. So be sure to think of your self as anything BUT a salesperson. You are much more than that and it is in your own conception of who you are that you will find your true value. When you discover how valuable you are and how valuable your ideas and concepts and abilities to engineer deals are, you will be able to command just about any level of profit you want out of any deal you put together.

But it starts and ends with you.

The power we have all been given by our Creator is the power of free will. It is the power to make choices. While we have all made unwise choices from time to time, the choice was ours to take. In most cases it was not thrust upon us usually, unless it was a job loss due to economic turbulence.

In business, the right choice is usually the hardest choice. Character and ethics play prominent roles. By always putting your best and highest efforts forward to benefit your clients, you really can't lose. This is the one choice no one can take from you - you have complete control over how to conduct your business and how you value your treasured clients.

You cannot always control your circumstances.
You cannot control other people.
You cannot control the economy.

But you CAN control how you **react** to your circumstances, other people and, yes, even the economy.

May God bless you.

Chapter Eight
More Resources for Tough Times

Home Staging for Profit

If you've already taken an expensive seminar, don't read this. It will break your heart. Best selling author and national trainer, Barbara Jennings has written an excellent guide on how to earn up to $100,000 or more from a home staging business. Director of the Academy of Staging and Redesign (Decorate-Redecorate.Com), she takes readers step by step through the maze of starting and growing a lucrative staging business, covering virtually everything one needs to know and more. She explores, explains and illustrates top business efforts, activities and opportunities. With decades of experience in staging and home business development, her large format manual teaches the essential tactics and strategies so anyone can succeed who puts forth the effort. Holding nothing back, she inspires and makes readers feel and sense they can and will do extraordinary things. It's loaded with numerous check lists, a wide variety of forms, over 140 pictures, specific how-to details and much more. Comprehensive dual certification courses for the most ambitious students, including visual aids and tools, are also available from the author's website.

For anyone who loves decorating and working with people, staging continues to be a fast growing industry with great profit potential no matter what the economic climate or where one lives. It combines decorating techniques with real estate strategies so stagers can effectively help owners sell their homes in record time for record profits, a vital service needed today more than ever. Written in a personable and conversational style, this guide is a must read for anyone serious (or just exploring). Photos help capture the essence of staging while giving readers a clear idea of what to expect. No degree or prior experience is needed. The manual exemplifies solid business training plus decorating and staging specifics, including:

- numerous candid before and after pictures of actual, recent projects
- the top mistakes and common problems sellers make
- what stagers must do and understand
- how to identify a home's assets and faults
- how to interview and bond with real estate agents
- how to interview and bond with home owners
- the five ingredients for a successful staging service
- professional image, attitudes and ethics needed
- how to do consultations, submit bids, make presentations
- how to set up the business, licenses to get and so forth
- how to get clients and referrals from multiple sources
- how to profit from consultations and offer full staging services
- how to promote, maintain and sustain the business indefinitely
- how to price services with confidence and ease
- how to protect, organize and prioritize
- 47 staging tricks for instant home appeal
- 107 questions to ask agents and homeowners to help quote services
- detailed pricing guidelines for furnished and empty houses
- legal issues readers should know about
- extensive list of stager tools needed for actual projects
- extensive cleaning and painting guidelines
- a 29-page detailed checklist to make consultations easy
- list of over 300 possible business names
- detailed information on available visual aids, promotional tools, management tools, and dual certification courses, which were pre-developed to supplement reader's knowledge, increase confidence and hone design skills are also included

Bonus Section includes:

- 15 handy reproducible forms ready to go
- multiple checklists and handout examples for value added services

For more details, please visit:
http://www.decorate-redecorate.com/home-staging-training.html

Getting Paid: Financial Strategies for Home Stagers

Do you make these mistakes when home staging? Many stagers unwittingly set themselves up for failure when it is so easy to avoid. If you've ever lost money on a project or you're afraid you might one day, this guide is for you. Best selling home staging author, Barbara Jennings, provides another excellent strategy-filled plan, with insider secrets, to generate and protect your profits every step of the way. There are times when clients look to escape paying for their services and home stagers need to be prudent and savvy to avoid such unfair practices. This guide teaches concrete, specific steps to take to make sure the proper documents and paper trails have been initiated to insure full payment once projects are completed. While no one wants to have to sue a client, this sometimes becomes necessary and readers will learn specific steps to take in advance to ward off the need for court, but at the same time protect their interests should legal recourse become necessary. This explicit guide also provides **53 fresh illustrated staging "tricks"** to enhance your services while making a property look spectacular. This section alone is well worth the price of the guide.

For detailed information, please visit:
http://www.decorate-redecorate.com/getting-paid.html

Staging Luxurious Homes

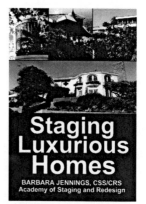

Get the secrets to profiting from the rich and famous in your neighborhood, town or city. Now at last readers get to peer into the benefits and strategies of building a home staging clientele among the rich and famous. While the spending habits of lower demographic groups is being adversely affected and cut back by the current recession, lack of available credit and job losses, affluent populations are often less affected or have better means of sustainability and adaptability. Designing a business for wealthy clients is one way to lower risk today and build for tomorrow at the same time. This guide shows readers how to transition their business to reach the top wealth earners and network among the leaders and pillars of their community with ease and confidence.

Top home staging and interior redesign expert, Barbara Jennings of Decorate-Redecorate.Com, teaches you the best and most efficient ways to locate and attract a luxurious homeowner as a client. Readers will learn how to network with wealthy, highly successful homeowners and professionals and how to profit with their services in upscale communities. Anyone can specialize in the affluent market with the proper training. Profits generally are dramatically higher for the same time and effort. Learn how to assist the top real estate agents and their wealthier homeowners by using design and organizational skills geared to promote faster home sales for higher prices. Topics included in the book are:

- Who Are the Affluent?
- How Do the Affluent Think and Feel?
- Where to Find the Affluent
- Networking with the Affluent
- When to Contact the Affluent
- How to Contact the Affluent
- How to Attract the Affluent
- Selling to the Affluent
- Pricing to the Affluent
- Serving the Affluent
- Avoiding the Pseudo-Affluent
- Becoming Affluent Yourself
- The Path to Becoming Affluent
- Plus Bonus Section

Written in a no-nonsense, conversational style, Staging Luxurious Homes is not a coffee table book filled with pictures of wealthy homes. Rather it teaches readers (who want a thriving home staging or interior re-design business) how to market specifically to upscale clients who can easily afford their services and who tend to associate with other upscale homeowners. This detailed, straight-talking guide is the 4th in a series by Jennings.

In Staging Luxurious Homes, readers will learn all the necessary and productive steps they should take to network with wealthy homeowners, gain access to a long networking list, be privy to special trade discounts from national providers of staging props, home accessories and much more. Readers will also learn how the wealthy think, when they make major buying decisions, how to approach them and earn their trust, other powerful do's and don'ts and much more.

For detailed information, please visit:
 http://www.decorate-redecorate.com/staging-luxurious-homes.html

Staging Portfolio Secrets

IS YOUR PORTFOLIO PICTURE POOR? Why do some people almost always make money in home staging or interior redesign while others struggle? Do your efforts to promote your services "implode" during the presentation? Are you always losing out to your competitors? At last help for struggling home stagers and re-designers has arrived. These are visual businesses, so it behooves consultants to develop a strong portfolio that speaks favorably about their talent, their knowledge, their expertise, their background and their uniqueness. This is no easy task.

Staging Portfolio Secrets helps readers pull out their strengths, gather powerful statistics about themselves, pull together distinctive photos to highlight their talents and display critical information to impress the most discerning prospects. Don't let your portfolio destroy your confidence and opportunities for success. Learn the secrets the most successful consultants don't want you to know. Make every prospect believe in you and trust you immediately. Watch your business grow and your referrals explode.

Now you can take your home staging and redesign business to much higher, bigger, better, more profitable yields or results by creating the professional credentials and visuals so vital to attracting new clients. Best selling author, Barbara Jennings, of the **Academy of Staging and Redesign** hosted at Decorate-Redecorate.Com reveals it all. To build a large clientele takes a thought provoking, visual presentation so that potential clients can see and understand the many talents and services the consultant offers. Great presentations do the work for you but only if they incorporate the right types of information and highlight your personal strengths and attributes. Staging Portfolio Secrets identifies, addresses and explains the following topics: Secrets to building a six figure home staging and redesign business; Discovering your accomplishments and defining them with power; New ways of thinking in the 21st century; Keys to success and door bangers that lead to failure; Pulling together your strengths in compelling ways; Pulling together your biographical information in succinct ways; Writing copy that sells your talents so you don't have to; The all important referral letter - how to write it and how to use it; Getting past the gatekeeper and to the top real estate agents, home owners and executives; Preparing for the interviews and how to present yourself boldly; The referral interview that leads to new clients; Dress codes for interviews - what works and what to avoid; Interpreting face language so you can adapt to others instantly; Tips for photos and more; How to shoot the best, most effective photos; Using humor in your presentations; Getting testimonials and Letters of Reference; Using success stories effectively; How to use your portfolio effectively and efficiently; Presentation cases; Layout and design ideas; Using the web to promote your portfolio; 16 useful forms for consultations and testimonials; Bonuses and Concluding Remarks

By understanding and following the concepts and precepts outlined in this guide, readers will be empowered to create brilliant presentations second to none that highlight and showcase their talents, knowledge and experience. In an ever increasingly competitive world, this guide will help readers zero in on talents and expertise they don't even know they have so that regardless of their experience, they will be able to impress anyone who sees their portfolio. As always, the author's writing style is personable and conversational and the perfect complement to other training she has offered to home stagers, giving them every upside advantage in the marketplace.

For detailed information, please visit:
 http://www.stagingportfoliosecrets.com

Rearrange It!

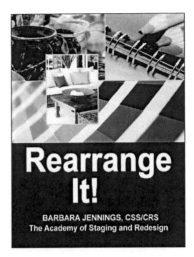

Does it drive you crazy to go into someone's home and see everything in the wrong place? Do you constantly want to rearrange your furniture? Would you like to make outstanding money arranging furniture and accessories for others? Interior Redesign is the creative use of professional furniture and accessory "arrangement" techniques to transform a client's home from ordinary into extraordinary by moving and arranging the furniture and accessories the client already owns. It is one of the easiest and most rewarding businesses in the design field today. Now Barbara Jennings, the West Coast pioneer of interior redesign, offers readers a way to improve, enhance, enrich and dramatically grow their income with their own home based redesign business. No experience necessary - no degree necessary.

As director of the Academy of Staging and Redesign, Jennings explains the best, easiest and most profitable ways to start, grow, manage and sustain a highly successful redecorating business. She brings 37 years of experience in home business development together with decades of interior design expertise in this large format, practical manual that reveals in simple terms the how-to strategies of top professional re-designers. She teaches readers exactly what to say and do on their half day or full day projects. A very simple, low risk business to learn, readers will discover how to transform a home in a matter of hours using just what is there, then making suggestions as to what additional products and services the homeowner could acquire, if needed. The manual provides business set-up and superb marketing training, as well as design training, and the author suggests plenty of additional training and visual aids that could be acquired which will be helpful to readers as they build their business and market their services to consumers. Readers will learn to integrate, advance and deploy workable, sustainable methods that lead to confidence, empowerment and strong profits, even in a tough economy.

Written in a no-nonsense, yet personable style, **Rearrange It!** will teach readers, who want a thriving interior redesign business:

- how to prepare themselves professionally
- how to get clients and referrals
- how to conduct consultations the right way
- how to set up their business and protect themselves legally
- how to hang art and pictures properly
- how to market and promote their services in a variety of ways
- how to get free publicity for their business
- and so much more

Readers will also learn:

- how to reach potential clients and qualify them
- how to assess a room quickly and know how to solve the problems
- 31 examples of arrangement techniques used by professionals (including the most popular furniture arrangement configurations, one of which should solve even the most complicated room)
- 20 questions to ask homeowners before starting a redesign consult
- practical do's and don'ts
- questions and answers
- important legalities and set up guidance
- how to develop a business plan
- the proper business etiquette
- an extensive furniture and accessory moving tips segment
- how to charge for services
- how to get referrals and testimonials
- how to get other tools and resources she has created to help promote and manage the business
- and how to get free ongoing training via her monthly newsletters.

For detailed information, please visit:
 http://www.decorate-redecorate.com/rearrange.html

Advanced Redesign

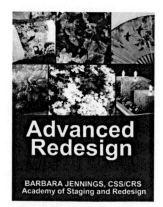

Get more activity, more power, more utilization, more efficiency, more mastery -- more of everything -- from the basic, universal concepts and stratagems used by the top re-designers, designers and home stagers in the industry.
One of the easiest and smartest ways to garner more clients and get the

maximum amount of profit out of the business relationship and get them to purchase more and to do so more often is to implement money-making multipliers, mechanisms and catalysts that offer great value and superior service to people who already trust you and have done business with you. This is the primary goal of **Advanced Redesign** - to show readers how to do exactly that. It's the additional, value-added products and services offered clients that separates one's business from the competition and propels it to the heights of income, gain preeminence in the area over all competitors. By incorporating correctly just a few of these ingenious gems, readers should enjoy improved, enhanced and enriched profits, greater variety and maximum enjoyment in their business.

Now staging and redesign expert Barbara Jennings teaches readers the best and most efficient ways to expand a home staging or interior re-design and redecorating business marketing a wide variety of natural backend products and services to appeal to a broader client base. Statistics prove that one's best, most lucrative business comes from current and former clients. This guide will help readers examine, evaluate, identify and observe areas they may not have thought about before. It will show how to integrate, advance and deploy these products and services.

Launching a basic home staging or interior re-design business is great, but stagers and re-designers can easily miss out on an abundance of extra profits by not offering related products and services to their clientele. By correcting these oversights, readers will have a much higher, bigger, better, more profitable yield or result from their marketing efforts. Jennings offers you a myriad of standard and "not so standard" ideas to help expand one's business in a professional manner. A sequel to her other top guides for the home staging and redesign industries, this large sized manual is brimming with advanced tactics and strategies.

Written in a serious yet conversational style, **Advanced Redesign** teaches anyone who wants to earn maximum profits from their business how to add strategic products and services that will help their clients beyond arranging their furniture and accessories or sprucing up their house. This thorough, idea-driven guide is the 3rd in a series by Jennings. It takes the reader deeper and more creatively into strategies and tactics they should consider adding to their basic services that are creative, enjoyable and highly profitable. With these varied ideas, readers can pick and choose what best works for them based on their personal interests, background, locality, competitive edge and experience.

For detailed information, please visit:
 http://www.decorate-redecorate.com/advanced-redesign.html

Dual Certification Courses in Home Staging and Redesign to Fast-track Your Way to Success

After 7 years of development, we are pleased to inform readers that we have the most comprehensive home study courses in the industry, bar none. Our courses include a combination of learning methods: ebooks, manuals and member's only website. In addition they provide students with actual promotional aids and tools of the trade to assist not only with promoting their businesses in professional and visual ways, but assist in moving heavy furniture and other important aspects of both businesses.

Courses also include the ability to enter our certification process to achieve our highly coveted and respected designations. They also include lifetime listings in our professional directories, postcards, websites and personal web pages, videos of one's early work, a discussion forum, monthly newsletters and email advice and support. Please note that many of the components that comprise a course may also be purchased "a la carte" and that students can upgrade to a course or a higher level of course and receive credits or substitutions by contacting our office.

Please visit our website for more specifics on the current courses, pricing, contact information and all the details: www.decorate-redecorate.com.

Design Training Galore

Our core design training for home staging and redesign is given to students through our electronic ebook called **Décor Secrets Revealed**. This is a comprehensive look at the secret techniques designers use to professionally arrange furniture and accessories. It is loaded with hundreds of full color images and is 25 chapters devoted to virtually everything you need to know on design as it applies to staging and redesigning homes.

It is highly recommended to take this training. When you're working for a client, they will have questions. You want to have instant, authoritative answers for them based on solid design concepts accepted everywhere as the standard. This training comes automatically in every course we offer but can also be purchased "a la carte" as well. There are over 600 images in the ebook. You must read it on your computer, but it is a pleasurable, easy breezy read and has received rave reviews.

For more details, please visit:
http://www.decorate-redecorate.com/decor.html

Wall Groupings!
Learn the Secrets of Displaying Your Art & Photos for Your Clients

This handy exclusive book of ours will teach you virtually everything you need to know to create beautiful arrangements using your client's art or photos. You won't need it for staging, but you will definitely benefit from this training if you are doing redesign.

It is the sequel to Barb's former popular book named Where There's a Wall – There's a Way which was originally published in the 1980s. The new book is updated and shows picture after picture of successful arrangements to stimulate your own personal creativity. It also shows you some failed examples to help you learn what works and what doesn't and why. For more details, please visit:
http://www.decorate-redecorate.com/book.html

Steel Furniture Lifter with Carpet Sliders and Floor Sliders Make Moving Furniture Super Easy

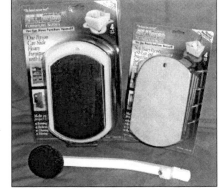

Professional stagers and re-designers never leave home without taking their tools. Moving furniture can be extremely difficult and back breaking unless you have the proper tools. By using the furniture lifter in combination with the sliders, you'll quickly discover you can move virtually any piece of furniture all by yourself without effort and without pain.

Most professionals carry several sets of sliders with them to appointments because it is much easier and quicker to be able to move several pieces of furniture without having to remove and replace the sliders from one piece to another. No self respecting stager or re-designer should be without these tools. You can buy the set and also buy extra sliders at our website.

For details, please visit:
http://www.decorate-redecorate.com/furniture-lifter.html

Home Staging Showcase Book Makes Excellent Presentations for You

You can call this many different things from your personal portfolio to a career showcase book to your talent book – whatever you call it, it is your visual presentation that you use to demonstrate to prospects the benefits of having their home staged by a professional. While we recognize that the most effective books or binders or folders are ones created by the individual consultant using their own photos as proof of their talent and success, when you're new you don't have the necessary ingredients to put one together that represents you in a professional manner. Thankfully you don't have to suffer as a result because we were the first to create one for students and you can get ours and use it as long as you like. Ours is 28 full color pages with lots of handsome photos and explanations of why hiring the services of a home stager is so important – just long enough to tantalize your prospects and not bore them. Labels are provided for you to designate your ownership of the book. Until such time as you get a body of your own work together to show to your prospects, use our Staging Showcase Book. NOTE: This is not a coffee table book - it is specifically for your private presentation of the benefits of home staging and redesign to your prospects.

For details, visit:
http://www.homestagingshowcase.com

Consultation Guides for Fast and Easy Consults

Doing consultations is hectic and nerve racking enough without the added pressure of having to take notes and go back to your home office to prepare documents for a client. It's all so unnecessary anyway. So to shortcut all that hassle and time consuming nonsense, we've created the first ever consultation booklet that you can use on the spot to do every consultation you run across. Each guide is written to the home owner, just in case they are going to do the work of staging themselves. The professional stager uses the booklet while on the consult, then either keeps the booklet as a guide to stage the home or provides the guide to the owner as part of the consultation fee. Either way the cost is always passed on to the client so the guides are <u>free</u> to the stager. We sell them in small quantities from the website. These 80-page checklists of the most typical tasks a stager needs to address take all the uncertainty and effort out of doing consultations.

For details, please visit:
http://www.decorate-redecorate.com/home-staging-for-yourself.html

Look Professional With Our Organizer Bag with 3 Insert Dividers

Many professionals also offer shopping services to their clients. This handsome, sophisticated organizer can replace your purse or briefcase. It comes with 3 organizational inserts that help you keep all your client's swatches and samples, all invoices and measurements and literally everything you need for your projects completely organized and handy. These are just some of the many, many tools at your disposal to help you organize, manage and grow your business. Additional dividers available direct from manufacturer.

For more details, please visit:
http://www.decorate-redecorate.com/decorating-shopper.html

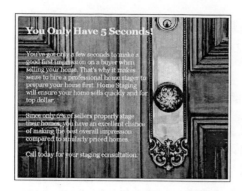

Promotional Aids Are Great!

Home staging and redesign are visual businesses and you cannot expect to properly or effectively promote and market your business without good visual aids. Postcards are just one of many ways to inexpensively get the word out and keep in touch with your prospects and clients.

While we're not in the business of providing printing services for students, we do offer some beautiful full color starter postcards to help you get launched quickly and effectively. We have several styles with strong sales messages available at our website. Come take a peek.

For details, please visit:
http://www.decorate-redecorate.com/postcards.html

A La Carte Aids, Tools, Apparel and More

We offer students many, many different aids to assist in starting, growing, managing, organizing and promoting a business in our industry. For a complete list of currently available products, please visit our shopping cart catalog.

http://www.decorate-redecorate.com/catalog.html

Review From Interior Designer

"Please accept my sincere gratitude. Your books (which I recently ordered and read) are absolutely packed with information. I've been a practicing interior designer for the past few years and decided recently to add staging to my services; my degree is in Interior Design but many of the items you present in your books are not addressed in college programs. There were several books/classes that I considered but in all my research your name came up repeatedly as the best "no-nonsense, down-to-earth, frank" staging book. I have spent a substantial amount of money on classes, books and webinars over the years and what you provide is worth far more than what you charge. Many thanks!"

Ruxana Oosman, Allied Member, ASID, Ruxana's Home Interiors

TESTIMONIAL "Again, thank you so much for all your wonderful training you have put together. I am in the process of re-reading everything because I am picking up different things this time around now that I have been out there and tried a few projects. You have so much more detailed helpful information than any other materials I have purchased. I am so excited about my new career!!! - Victoria Guillett"

TESTIMONIAL "I was working with one home, and when I was looking to rent furniture the person at the place of my choosing asked where I was getting my certification from. After I mentioned your name and program, she said that she has worked with 2 other individuals from your program. And, she thought very highly of the work being done by these people. Just thought you'd like to know that! - Debi Wheatley"

TESTIMONIAL "I feel that the training has been excellent. I think the material is concise and covers the information that a stager and re-designer should know and that the challenges I might encounter have been addressed. I feel the course was thorough and complete. I would like to add, however, that reading Chapter 25 in Décor Secrets Revealed was an additional confirmation for me that I had purchased the right course. The feelings expressed by Barbara Jennings parallel my own; I was truly divinely guided to make the right decision. - Karen Yore (Diamond Trainee)"

TESTIMONIAL "Hi Barbara, . . . Business is good - even given tough times. I continue to partner with local realtors and have built an excellent customer base for both staging and design just from referrals. Hope all is well, Dori Curtis, CSS/CRS Interior Staging and Design"

TESTIMONIAL "I'm barely into it, but it's already gotten me back to feeling excited about the possibilities. – Mama Red "Shopper" (Brooklyn)"

TESTIMONIAL ". . . Barbara is not trying to impress people with her credentials, she is trying to help them with her experience! If you are considering staging for a living – get this book! – Mark A Hoyt (Greenville, SC)"

Contact the Author

Academy of Staging and Redesign
Decorate-Redecorate.Com
Box 2632, Costa Mesa, CA 92628-2632   (714) 963-3071
support3@barbarajennings.com

Breinigsville, PA USA
30 March 2011

258771BV00001BA/48/P